The Rhythm of Images

A Cultural Critique Book

Cesare Casarino, John Mowitt, and Simona Sawhney, Editors

THE RHYTHM OF IMAGES

CINEMA BEYOND MEASURE

DOMIETTA TORLASCO

A Cultural Critique Book

University of Minnesota Press
Minneapolis
London

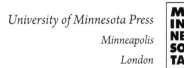

An earlier version of chapter 4 was published as "Photography as Rhythm: On Victor Burgin's *Prairie*," in *Seeing Degree Zero: Barthes/Burgin and Political Aesthetics,* ed. Ryan Bishop and Sunil Manghani (Edinburgh: Edinburgh University Press, 2019), 393–412.

Copyright 2021 by the Regents of the University of Minnesota

All rights reserved. No part of this publication may be reproduced, stored in a retrieval system, or transmitted, in any form or by any means, electronic, mechanical, photocopying, recording, or otherwise, without the prior written permission of the publisher.

Published by the University of Minnesota Press
111 Third Avenue South, Suite 290
Minneapolis, MN 55401-2520
http://www.upress.umn.edu

ISBN 978-1-5179-1020-4 (hc)
ISBN 978-1-5179-1021-1 (pb)

Library of Congress record available at https://lccn.loc.gov/2020058499

Printed in the United States of America on acid-free paper

The University of Minnesota is an equal-opportunity educator and employer.

Contents

	Acknowledgments	vii
	Introduction	1
1	Life	13
2	Labor	39
3	Memory	71
4	Medium	99
	Notes	127
	Index	155

Acknowledgments

I have often thought of film editing as a kind of dancing. So if this book on montage ended up revolving around images of dancers, luminous and unruly, it also came into being by virtue of the friends and colleagues who joined me in that dance with the pen—the echo of the films' own dancing—that I was attempting to practice. My gratitude goes to Cesare Casarino, whose writings on cinema rekindled my passion for thinking in images and sounds, inspiring me to compose the video essay *Philosophy in the Kitchen* (2014), and whose friendship and intellectual generosity have punctuated my life since; Brian Price, whose work in film philosophy has been a constant companion in my research and whose friendship has kept alive my belief in thinking-together; Tiziana Terranova, a longtime and ever-present friend whose intellectual determination always helps me go where I am headed, even before I know it myself; the editors of *Cultural Critique,* John Mowitt, Cesare Casarino, and Simona Sawhney, who welcomed my book in their series and offered precious feedback as it was taking shape; Ryan Bishop and Sanil Manghani, who first responded to my writing experiments on rhythm; the University of Minnesota Press readers, Brian Price and James Cahill, whose intellectual openness and insightfulness I can only hope to emulate; the University of Minnesota Press editors Danielle Kasprzak, Jason Weidemann, and Leah Pennywark, who supported the publication of this book with resolve and professionalism, and their editorial assistant, Anne Carter, who smoothed out all transitions; Tess Cavagnero, who prepared the manuscript for publication with the unique precision of a classics scholar; and, last but not least, Kyle Kaplan, whose knowledge of music theory and interpretive sensitivity played a pivotal role in honing my analysis of the films' acoustic landscapes. The Kaplan Institute for the Humanities at Northwestern University, where I was a fellow in the 2018–19 academic year, provided me with institutional support and a forum for sustained exchange.

This book is dedicated to Beppe and Mariagrazia, my parents; and to Matteo, Diletta, and Alberto.

Introduction

Cinema is by now very old. It might even already be dead. Yet screen images continue to permeate our lives and they do so with a vengeance, a sense of relentless anticipation that too often stifles creativity. What I have in mind is first of all the creativity of spectatorship, the capacity to remain open to a life of images that exceeds the parameters of our embodied experience. I understand this experience to be utterly technical, so I am concerned less with the transition to the digital than with the loss of a certain imaginative receptivity, what Walter Benjamin called "room-for-play," as it connects to a neoliberal appropriation of media.[1] The stakes in an aesthetics of play that favors *paidia* over *ludus,* improvisation over regulation, are ontological: at its most radical, the inventiveness of play engenders configurations that redraw the lines of our relationship with the world and its depth of space and time. Neither properly internal nor external, the life of images that cinema has produced during its brief life and prolonged death has now acquired a renewed ghostly luminosity and, with it, the power to demand more life. "I want more life, fucker," says Roy Batty to his corporate maker in Ridley Scott's *Blade Runner* (1982). That the last bit is dubbed as "father" in the unrated version only contributes to disclose the symbolic matrix of the cyborg's living death. At the same time, the cyborg points to a domain in which borders and hierarchies have already been meddled with and bodies no longer "end at the skin, or include at best other beings encapsulated by skin."[2]

Years ago I reedited Dorothy Malone's frenzied dance in Douglas Sirk's

Written on the Wind (1956), producing a drawn-out whirlpool of red fabric in low-definition digital video. The clip became part of a short proposal for a new erotics of vision, a sort of comet tail to Maurice Merleau-Ponty's *The Visible and the Invisible* and the attempt to explore the erotics of the flesh—Merleau-Ponty's term for the coiling over of the visible on itself—as an erotics of potentiality. I realize now that, by reframing and slowing down fragments of genre films, I was pursuing a kind of "acinematic" rewriting of movement, one that would allow images to return on themselves gratuitously or, rather, without end. Jean-François Lyotard calls this betrayal of purposefulness "sterile motion" and presents the following scene as an example:

> A match once struck is consumed. If you use the match to light the gas that heats the water for the coffee which keeps you alert on your way to work, the consumption is not sterile, for it is a movement belonging to the circuit of capital . . . But when a child strikes the matchhead *to see* what happens—just for the fun of it—he enjoys the movement itself, the changing colors, the light flashing at the height of the blaze, the death of the tiny piece of wood, the hissing of the tiny flame. He enjoys these sterile differences leading nowhere, these uncompensated losses; what the physicist calls the dissipation of energy.[3]

I like this scene for several reasons: it turns to cinema as a medium that gives us room to play with forms and their intensity; it hosts, perhaps unwillingly, some residual narrative traits; and it eschews repetition as the return of the same, that is, of a difference caught in a system of equivalences. All in all, in the context of Lyotard's "philosophy of cinema," this scene may be taken to express the notion of a general rather than restricted economy, in keeping with Georges Bataille's critique of capitalism. What it describes is a resistance or even indifference to a logic of exchange that is at work not only in the domain of economics proper but also in the interrelated domains of kinship, language, and sexuality. Jean-Joseph Goux would call these economies *symbolic*, as they all rely on a principle of substitution (metaphor is never far away) that requires the positing of a standard measure or *general equivalent* according to which equivalence between entities can be established.[4] The contemporary vicissitudes of measure have complicated the general economy of this scenario, yet let me begin by suggesting that the contrast between Lyotard's expenditure and the "fecundity" of

Merleau-Ponty's flesh be treated as an imperfect superimposition. It is the very sterility of certain perceptual differences, their indifference to telos and profit, that renders them at once valueless and invaluable—the sign of a perverse productivity, achieved without proper bodily organs or even proper bodies, a productivity without end.

If I linger on these differences and the small conflagration or pyrotechnical event that expresses them, it is because Lyotard goes on to indicate that it is a question of rhythm. While discussing repetition as the return of the same, he addresses "the folding back of diversity into identical unity" as it occurs in painting with plastic and chromatic patterning, in music with the resolution of dissonance, in architecture with proportion.[5] In cinema, it is hardly surprising to hear that plot is sovereign and cinematography orders the perceptual field by excluding erratic movements, to the extent that even interruptions or jolts in continuity are ultimately recuperated as "beneficial detours."[6] Lyotard calls these ostensible disturbances "arrhythmias," confirming his alignment of rhythm with cohesion and, in this case at least, his propensity for treating narrative cinema as a playground for normalization.[7] And yet, can we look at the scene of the child and the match as something other than an arrhythmia, albeit one that resists being reclaimed? That is, can we conceive of a rhythm that, in itself, makes visible what is "nonrecurrent," that affirms difference as primary and absolute? The child's burning flame, perhaps also Malone's flaring nightgown, would then be engendering not only "a disconcerted body, invited to stretch its sensory capacities beyond measure," but also a volatile body—a configuration of which flesh, fire, and celluloid all momentarily partake.[8] Indeed, the rhythm which I am attempting to tackle is not on the side of the spectator any more than it is on the side of the film; it does not belong to the rustling match any more than it does to the child holding it. It is the fleeting, erratic configuration of child and fire, nightgown and spectator, as it modulates the perceptual field anew, experimenting with its texture without weaving in patches of self-identical design. The configuration is its own monstrous corporeality.

In *The Rhythm of Images,* I take up the challenge of thinking rhythm as a mode of being in the sensible—*of* the sensible—that is informed by radical difference. I begin by proposing that we consider this rhythm as a form of life, singular and self-differing, a mode of being that challenges both the logic of measure according to which subjects and objects have long been produced—in markets and families, as commodities and concretions of desire—and what seems to be its opposite, a propagation of dismeasure that harnesses the potential of perception without releasing it. In this respect, I share in what Antonio Negri has called "the hope for and choice of a life that is not hierarchically ordered or prefigured by forms of measure," although I am not as ready as he is to declare that the immeasurable, the "outside measure" through which Empire now rules, has not also pervasively affected the very subjectivity of the multitude, draining their capacity to act "beyond measure," through novel systems of capture.[9] The suspicion, at least vis-à-vis our new screen society, is that power has recloaked its standards, even inverted their sign, instead of simply abandoning them. In this landscape, the rhythm I pursue is a matter of ontological force—indeed an arrangement of matter, the temporary form that atoms take, as we will soon see. It is *beyond* measure" not because it points to a transcendent domain but, rather, because it springs out of and inhabits the internal dehiscence of perception, its immanent excess or potential. As such, this rhythm beyond measure does not mark a barrier or limit to be surpassed (only to be renewed and surpassed again), according to a logic that still bears the imprint of the quantitative. On the contrary, it coincides with a leap into quality, tentative, intermittent—it does not matter whether fast or slow, abrupt or discreet—a leap that can be said to occur here and now provided that we renounce any punctual determination of time and space and instead immerse ourselves in duration.

From the start, my argumentation unfolds through the mutual reworking of cinematic fragments and theoretical texts. As in my previous book, *The Heretical Archive*, I repeatedly privilege fragments over authors or genres, and open trajectories over taxonomies. I speak of histories always to come and to be written collectively, in a process of archival reinvention rather than completed tasks. It would thus be impossible to disentangle and place along a progressive line the two main objectives of this work: to elaborate a notion of rhythm that prioritizes difference and to trace the contours of an image practice that resists our ongoing depletion of the sensible. In the first case, I begin by attending to Émile Benveniste's interpretation of the Greek term *rhuthmos* (rhythm) as a momentary, improvised form and its subsequent mobilization by Roland Barthes and Philippe Lacoue-Labarthe. These texts operate as the springboard for an inquiry into the role that rhythm plays in articulating the relationship between the aesthetic and the political. In the second case, I look back at Italian Neorealism and locate the emergence of a new rhythmic impulse at the heart of what is usually celebrated as a cinema of duration. This retrospective analysis is to be considered simultaneously with the investigation of works by Chantal Akerman, Michelangelo Antonioni, Victor Burgin, Harun Farocki, Jean-Luc Godard, David Lynch, and Jean Vigo, which I gather together in constellations that erode the subject of European cinema from within. With respect to both trajectories, the origin to which I return belongs to a futural past. The rhythms or configurations that I pursue are to be invented rather than found—invented as they are performed in a process of reviewing and rewriting. Indeed, regaining room-for-play not only in the practice but also in the theory of spectatorship might be one way of "reappropriat[ing] the potentiality of dismeasure."[10]

Let me briefly introduce the key term of this inquiry, *rhuthmos* (rhythm), which I adopt in the sense proposed by Émile Benveniste, and then qualify the modalities of my engagement with it. According to Benveniste, in pre-Socratic philosophy and in lyric and tragic poetry, *rhuthmos* named a passing, irregular form or configuration.[11] One could speak of rhuthmos in relation to the form of a letter, the arrangement of a garment, and even a disposition of the character or mood. Plato set rhythm in order, so to speak, by appropriating the term to define the movement of bodies in a dance according to a *metron* or external measure; thus normalized, rhythm could fulfill the aesthetic requirements of a unified political community. But before becoming "order in movement," rhythm was a "fluctuation," a form that does not coalesce, a "manner of flowing" that could be attributed to images, sounds, and affects alike. The implications of Benveniste's etymological recovery are manifold, and this book will address them in relation to four interrelated domains: life, labor, memory, and medium. At this juncture, I will simply note that, as interpreted by Benveniste, the term rhuthmos points to an arrangement that escapes the metaphysical opposition of form and matter; a configuration that is inseparable from the time of its appearance; a duration that is qualitative rather than quantitative; and an unmediated relationship between the political and the sensible.

Despite its complexity and potential reach, the notion of rhythm as rhuthmos has received relatively limited attention. The list of notable exceptions includes Roland Barthes, who devotes his 1977 lecture course *How to Live Together* to idiorrhythmy as the fantasy of a life that is at once singular and communal; Philippe Lacoue-Labarthe, who travels the farthest distance from the Lacanian mirror image and its aggressive rigidity when he turns to rhuthmos as a crucial trait in the "general differentiation of what is," including subjectivity; and Henri Meschonnic, for whom the bodily valence of rhythm enables the speaking subject to transform the very language by which it has been shaped.[12] In *A Thousand Plateaus*, Gilles Deleuze and Félix Guattari, too, refer to rhuthmos indirectly in a context that highlights the term's privileging of flow over stasis, fluctuation over solid form, quality over quantity. However, in their support of Michel Serres's *The Birth of Physics*, they attempt to make Benveniste say what he does not—namely, that rhythm is the "form of a 'measured, cadenced' movement."[13] In fact, Benveniste goes to great lengths to underscore that rhuthmos becomes a question of measurement and a determination of the human body only with Plato: "The decisive circumstance is there," he writes, "in the notion of a corporeal *rhuthmos* associated with *metron* and bound by the law of numbers: that 'form' is from then on determined by a 'measure' and numerically regulated."[14] What is at stake is not the subsequent distinction between rhythm and meter as it will preoccupy scholars of prosody and music, but this *other* life of rhythm—a virtual life, if you will, one in which the sensible eludes the power of counting, of thinking according to a standard. It would be impossible and quite beyond the point to pretend that the Platonic redefinition of rhythm did not occur; one can only write from within a certain history and yet can still attempt to write against it—that is, *for* something else. In their heterogeneity, all the interventions mentioned above engage with rhythm as *another* way of modulating life—the fantasy of life, the writing of life, the poetry of life, or, simply, "a life."[15]

As it returns throughout the book, rhuthmos does not present itself as a self-identical concept. What this other rhythm is and does mutates through displacements brought about by the encounter not only with multiple film fragments but also with different thinkers and fields of inquiry: Luce Irigaray and Giorgio Agamben in the first chapter; post-autonomist thought, Gilles Deleuze, and Italian feminism in the second; Walter Benjamin and his readers in the third; Sergei Eisenstein, Rosalind Krauss, and new theories of the border in the fourth. If I periodically return to Barthes and Lacoue-Labarthe's reading of Benveniste, it is because they untie the question of rhythm from that of music (or prosody, unlike Meschonnic), and do so in a movement of thought that challenges the self-sameness of the concept. On the one hand, then, it is in the wake of Lacoue-Labarthe's dispersion of arborescent thought and Barthes's non-method—"flitting, gleaning," as in Agnes Varda's archival journeys, with no preset destination or straight path—that I repeatedly turn to rhuthmos. On the other, rhuthmos becomes something different in each chapter: the form that life takes in a community that thrives on singularities; the form that time takes as it exceeds the constraints of labor time; a mode of remembrance that enables us to reimagine the past and envision fresh futures; a zone of aesthetic experimentation beyond the propriety of mediatic boundaries. All this is to say that I adopt a modified "theme-and-variation" structure, one in which the theme itself is but a variation, in order to enact my claim of rhuthmos as difference—to enact on a formal level what I describe on the level of content. Reiterations, returns, and resonances that lead "nowhere," if not into folds that do not fold back into themselves, are indispensable to my argument and its anti-economic drive.

The Rhythm of Images finds a kinship of trajectory in recent studies on aesthetics and ontology, most notably Souleymane Bachir Diagne's *African Art as Philosophy* and Jessica Wiskus's *The Rhythm of Thought*.[16] In both cases, the undoing of metaphysical dualities and the disengaging of time from measure emerge as inseparable from the intuition (Diagne) and the interrogation (Wiskus) of Being as rhythm. By following Léopold Sédar Senghor's adoption of Bergsonism, Diagne jointly claims rhythm as an ontological force and African art—in its very "*rhythmic* attitude"—as an ontology of vital forces. Here the privileging of "Being or rhythm or force" brings about forms of life in which the division between subject and object does not hold sway over experience, and "embrace-reason" (the opposite of "eye-reason") "dances rather than thinks the object."[17] Western culture itself is not immune from the breaking up of its own tradition, as it occurs with Henri Bergson's publication of *Time and Free Will*, which Senghor terms the "Revolution of 1889," and Arthur Rimbaud's "Lettres du voyant," the announcement of a trancelike poetry of the seer. While drawing on Merleau-Ponty, Wiskus, too, is interested in *voyance* as a "visioning" that exceeds metaphysical constraints, an experience in which time itself is seen rather than measured. In the folds of the perceptual world, she finds not subjects and objects but a modulation of Being as "inspiration and exhalation"—Being as rhythm. My project resonates with theirs and yet also distinguishes itself in its attempt to avoid the recuperation of any kind of unity (past or future, passing or lasting, plenary or divided). In both Diagne and Wiskus, rhythm allows for a dismantling of dualities but also precipitates a recovery of cohesion: what is lost at the level of subject and object is regained at the level of the texture into which they dissolve—that is, at the level of rhythm itself. While I cannot do justice to their nuanced arguments, let me touch on them, as it will help me make the case for an expanded notion of rhythm and, at the same time, elucidate the reasons for my commitment to rhuthmos as a notion that is to be created not just in the midst of, but actually by virtue of, unreconciled fragments.

The suggestion that, as an ontological force, rhythm is a matter of perceptual forms carries enormous weight. Diagne convincingly argues that the notion of a "*rhythmic* attitude" permeating African art finds a main source in Paul Guillaume and Thomas Munro's book *Primitive Negro Sculpture,* whose formalism is then reworked in light of Leo Frobenius's historical research. Senghor celebrates rhythm as "the vital element par excellence" and suggests that it relates to African sculpture as respiration does to life.[18] That, in an artwork, it expresses itself through oppositions of lines and colors does not make its pattern homogeneous: "reprise is not redundancy or repetition," and the theme or sculptural form always returns as a variation (296). However, this internal dynamism ultimately coincides with a tightly woven whole or a "unity in diversity": as a vital force, rhythm is an "ordering force."[19] Guillaume and Munro's formalism exercises its strongest influence at this juncture. If their assertion that an African statue is a "complete visual music" is more than a passing metaphor, it is because music functions as the guarantee of the artwork's cohesion. In other words, the rhythm of African art marks a break with the Western tradition of "eye-reason," and yet, by way of Guillaume and Munro, it still submits to unity as what supersedes multiplicity. I understand Diagne's point that, by claiming rhythm as an indivisible whole, Senghor is countering analytic reason and its drive toward dissection. But this whole, in the indivisibility of its nonetheless discrete parts, betrays the workings of a reason that has already divided the sensible according to a logic of identity.

The question of the priority conferred to identity over difference resurfaces in Wiskus's reading of Merleau-Ponty's ontology of the flesh as an ontology of rhythm. By turning to Stéphane Mallarmé, Paul Cézanne, Marcel Proust, and Claude Debussy, Wiskus attends to the complexity of Merleau-Ponty's notion of flesh and shows that—as the coiling over of the visible on itself and the invisible that constitutes its foil—the flesh can be thought rhythmically. The flesh's depth or latency pertains to not only space but also time: in the "mythical time" of a perception freed from perspective and chronology (like in the case of Cézanne's Mont Sainte Victoire or Proust's hawthorns), past and future encroach on each other, in a double, "outward and inward" movement of dispersion and concentration. As the chiasm of perception, the flesh of the world or flesh of time is itself rhythm. I am inspired by Wiskus's original interpretation and yet believe that, in straightforwardly asserting the flesh or rhythm as a "cohesion . . . of incompossibles," she reduces its indefinite productivity.[20] While building on Merleau-Ponty's assertion that "transcendence is identity within difference," she forgets to attend to the vicissitudes of the philosopher's language, the horizontal displacements through which he opens up the metaphors he employs.[21] This sliding prevents his descriptions from being held in a state of self-enclosed incompletion, a simultaneity that stifles difference. On the other hand, Wiskus tends to outline a telos and imprint a certain hierarchy there where a more elusive notion of the flesh is at work, a notion that is incessantly reworking the very language by which it is being worked over. Ultimately, Wiskus posits rhythm as the transcendence of the flesh, that is, "identity within difference." This claim does not simply take shape at the end but, as Wiskus skillfully performs the content of her argument, can already be found at the beginning, in the inaugural chapter on Mallarmé. The flesh of time as divergence—as the vortex of *voyance*—is caught in a circularity that has been closing on itself all along, so that becoming is reduced to the accord between past and future, simultaneity as cohesion.

What I consider invaluable in Wiskus's reading is that rhythm emerges *almost* as a form—almost but not quite. As an "element" of Being in the sense that water, air, earth, and fire were elements for pre-Socratic philosophy, the flesh performs a labor of differentiation that questions the dichotomy of form and matter without resorting to the concept of mediation. In this respect, by turning to rhuthmos as a fluctuation, I attempt to modify Ewa Plonowska Ziarek's call for a "new, interactive model of mediation between matter and form," one that could "account for . . . the violent schism between abstract forms and damaged materialities inflicted by modern biopolitics."[22] While I share her deep concern with the violence of political formalism, I believe that the concept of mediation still leaves too much of the metaphysics of the subject intact. It will then not come as a surprise that my project finds itself at a remote distance from Carole Levine's book, *Forms: Whole, Rhythm, Hierarchy, Network*. Levine's engagement with previous attempts at rethinking form, one in which Luce Irigaray, Fredric Jameson, Jacques Derrida, and Michel Foucault are collapsed together after having been perfunctorily given their due, betrays an investment in neutralizing difference that is in keeping with the overall argument she proposes. "It is the work of form to make order," she claims, in the same way as "sorting out what goes where" in space and time, to find the "proper places for bodies, goods, and capacities," is the work of politics.[23] The concept of "natural affordance" is offered here to account for an enormous range of phenomena (from novels to prisons to maternity leaves) and then validated on the basis of their recurrence. Indeed, even when a form is "put to use in unexpected ways," it is because those potentialities were already latent in the form itself, in a circuit of always predictable (and unavoidable) empty productivity.

This brief excursus into rigid formalism prompts me to clarify what I am not claiming. I am not claiming that rhuthmos always liberates, while other more conventional rhythms only constrain. Instead, I approach rhuthmos as a question that reformulates itself in the mutable configurations that it engenders, releasing a potential that is as much of the notion as it is of the sensible domain from which it emerges. This potential is ultimately the potential of life, of the resistance that life poses when it becomes the object of violence and exploitation.[24] To be sure, the book focuses on a particular kind of life—the life of images as it persists and renews itself in cinema's futural past. I borrow the expression "life of images" from Giorgio Agamben, who formulates it in relation to Aby Warburg's *Mnemosyne Atlas*. However, I develop it in a direction that exposes the dismissal—of flow, of duration—still lingering in Agamben's conception of time and shows that fluidity is not automatically synonymous with continuity or gradual, predictable becoming. Thus, in the first chapter, "Life," I explicitly address the long-standing dispute between form and flow while focusing on sequences from Farocki's *Bilder der Welt und Inschrift des Krieges* (*Images of the World and the Inscription of War*, 1988) and Vigo's *L'Atalante* (1934). By moving between Irigaray's critique of the subject, Lacoue-Labarthe's venture into a psychoanalysis of beatless rhythms, and Agamben's proposal for a modal ontology, I suggest that we look at cinematic rhuthmos as a form of life in which we partake, not as subjects or arrested images but as fluid traits.

In the second chapter, "Labor," I continue to investigate rhuthmos as a fluctuation by bringing together films that portray the confusion of life and labor, including the labor of filmmaking: Farocki's *Contre-chante* (*Counter-Music*, 2004), Vittorio De Sica's *Umberto D.* (1952), Akerman's *Jeanne Dielman, 23, Quai du Commerce, 1080 Bruxelles* (1975), and Godard's *Numéro deux* (*Number Two*, 1975). If Dziga Vertov's Человек с кино-аппаратом (*Man with a Movie Camera*, 1929) stands as the canonical point of reference for an inquiry in this field, I trace the emergence of irregular rhythmic clusters back to Italian Neorealism rather than the Russian Avant-garde, to the sphere of domestic rather than industrial labor: Akerman, Godard, and Farocki's figures connect most strongly not to Vertov's textile workers but to the young housemaid in *Umberto D.*, joining in her attempt to find more time in time, to inhabit a time that cannot be assimilated to money or exploitation. By rereading Gilles Deleuze's writings on cinema through the lens of Luisa Muraro, I propose that we reconceive of editing in relation to housework: not editing *as* housework, the work of metaphor, but editing *and* housework, the work of metonymy, here pushed to its limits and capable of producing disjunctions or fissures instead of associations.

In the third chapter, "Memory," I put to the test Bernard Stiegler's investment in the subject, now informed by technics but still conceived on the model of intentionality, as a means of resistance to our current symbolic misery. Turning back to Walter Benjamin's intervention in technical media, I reopen the question of technology and subjectivity with a novel interpretation of the aura as it emerges in narrative and essayistic cinema. In Godard's *Le Mépris* (*Contempt*, 1963) and Lynch's *Mulholland Drive* (2001), I maintain, the auratic returns as a rhythmic modulation of the sensible, a reconfiguration of color and lines that dissolves the divide between subject and object without flattening out time. In the deep time of memory, subject formation unfolds as a process of differentiation that is rhythmic and yet in excess of the beat or pulse—a process that occurs beyond the measure that has marked even our thought of the unconscious. Godard's *Le Livre d'image* (*The Image Book*, 2018) draws on the ontological force of this other rhythm to produce more radical effects, transforming us into constellations of flickering colors. Finally, in "Medium," I explore how the notion of rhuthmos can help us question the propriety of mediatic boundaries (between film, video, and photography) and their role in constraining our relationship to time as what we have most profoundly in common. At once far apart and contiguous, Victor Burgin's digital projections and Michelangelo Antonioni's *L'Eclisse* (*The Eclipse,* 1962) turn photography's alleged instantaneity into simultaneity as difference, the time of a shared and yet differentiated duration.

1. Life

OF FLUIDS

Harun Farocki's *Bilder der Welt und Inschrift des Krieges* (*Images of the World and the Inscription of War,* 1988), a film devoted to investigating the relations between vision, labor, and warfare, opens with images of a water research laboratory. A series of static shots registers the movement of waves as they are being produced in a long, white, plastered channel and then in a basin with a model boat. The sound of the waves and of the machinery generating them blends with the words spoken by a disembodied female voice: "When the sea surges against the land, irregularly, not haphazardly," she says, "this motion binds the look without fettering it and sets free the thoughts. The surge that sets the thoughts in motion is here being investigated scientifically in its own motion—in the large wave channel at Hannover." If the first sentence conjures up a scene of contemplation where the look is nonetheless acted on ("bound") by the movement that it takes as its object, the second sentence turns the water surge into a mere object of scientific observation, seemingly leaving no room for speculative play. Then the voice adds, "The motions of water are still less researched than those of light," anticipating the shift of emphasis—from water to light—that marks the rest of the film. The ensuing sequences are exemplary in this respect, as they bring together heterogeneous yet thematically coherent materials: the drawing of a powerful seeing eye from Albrecht Dürer's *Instruction in Measurement*; the spoken words "Enlightenment—that is a word in the history of ideas. In German: *Aufklärung*"; the close-up of a white woman's eye being professionally made up; and plates and original commentary documenting the invention of scale photography. All in all, *Bilder* presents us with nothing less than a veritable investigation of the field—at once aesthetic and political—in which vision articulates itself according to the divide between subject and object.

That *Bilder* does all this while constituting itself in defiance of such a model has been successfully argued by several scholars.[1] Still, when the opening sequence is addressed, it is remarked that it initially appears unmotivated or at odds with the film's associative network.[2] In other words, why images of water in a film that concerns itself primarily with photography as it relates to aerial warfare and metallurgic production? In *The Threshold of the Visible World*, Kaja Silverman suggests that, by virtue of the voice-over text and the lab setting, this sequence does in fact introduce the film's main oppositions, namely, the contrast "between scientific observation—which is here shown to involve a whole range of visual technologies—and the look, which, far from mastering its object, is itself implicated or 'tied up' with it."[3] I agree with Silverman on the sequence's role in establishing the opposition between quantitative and qualitative vision; I also take notice of the fact that she calls the latter "highly subjectivized" and identifies it with hand drawing. If *Bilder* stands as an example of cinematic resistance, it is because it comes closer to hand drawing in its capacity to maintain uncertain, blurred boundaries (against the clarity of police photography, for instance) and foster the workings of memory.[4] Yet I am not ready to leave the opening sequence behind, and neither is the film: in its apparent extraneity, the Hannover laboratory will appear again in the middle and near the end. The point is not that these images of water return but that they cannot be simply absorbed in or put at the service of the film's larger associative network. In fact, they spill out, disturbing its ostensible coherence, but also suggesting that the measurement of light might have begun with the binding of water.

Water is more than another kind of matter on which technology takes hold and imposes its rationality. One could say, following Luce Irigaray, that what is being displaced from here—flow, turbulence, impermanence—is nothing less than the constitutive outside of a theory and practice of vision that, in keeping with Western metaphysics, privileges form over matter, mind over body, male over female. In "The 'Mechanics' of Fluids" and "Volume without Contours," Irigaray develops a feminist critique of science and its reliance on formal logic's principles of negation, identity, and generality.[5] Specifically, she alerts us to the *"complicity of long standing between rationality and a mechanics of solids alone"*: not only has science confronted fluids belatedly but it has also reduced their complex dynamics by making them conform to solids.[6] This "'inattention' to fluids" has marked the history of both physics and metaphysics. Fluids—"blood but also milk, sperm, lymph, spittle, saliva, tears, humours, gasses, waves, air, fire"—are always in excess with respect to unity and self-sameness and the system of symbolization that sanctions them; they are also *"in excess with respect to form,"* at least to the extent that the latter has been "solidified" and made to coincide with sharp and stable contours, turned into a geometric or ideal form.[7] For Irigaray, "woman" embodies and speaks this turbulence, being "never one, male or female"; always in the process of becoming other, inhabiting a temporality that cannot be reduced to any simple present; "overflowing," "fluctuating," "blurring."[8] Psychoanalysis, too, has adopted a *"mechanics of near-solids,"* relegating the properties of fluids to the "feminine" and positing a subject that protects himself from dissolving into it through the solidity of form.[9] So in Jacques Lacan's discourse, for instance, we find an economy of desire that, at the level of the symbolic, revolves around the signification of the phallus (metaphor being farther from fluidity and propagation than metonymy) and, at the level of the imaginary, privileges the Gestalt of the mirror image, no matter how fictional it is supposed to be. But, in order for the subject to entertain the illusion of his consistency, "all water must become a mirror, all seas, a glass."[10]

Irigaray's critique is at once scathing and dispersed, radically elliptical in her mode of argumentation (for instance, she omits names and simply encourages the reader to research the history of solid and fluid mechanics; Lacan, too, is mentioned explicitly only in a footnote). N. Katherine Hayles attempts to fill in these lacunae by examining foundational theories of hydraulics and addressing the role that a male imaginary has played in their development. The basic hierarchical dichotomies she identifies, "continuity versus rupture" and "conservation versus dissipation," seem to confirm Irigaray's claims. However, in her decision to engage with "the rules of scientific discourse," Hayles ends up reaffirming some of their pitfalls, even reformulating Irigaray's own argument in the language of analogy.[11] But Irigaray, who wants to sabotage "time-honored devices such as analogy, comparison, symmetry, dichotomous oppositions," posits no simple analogy between women and fluidity; rather, she exposes and undermines the way this trope has been constituted.[12] In "Toward a Radical Female Imaginary," Ewa Plonowska Ziarek shows that the charge of essentialism, strategic or otherwise, that has characterized the reception of Irigaray's work on fluidity and embodiment can be related to the fact that "most [readers] consider this fluidity as either a 'literal' or 'figurative' attribute of the sexed body rather than an effect of the temporal structure of becoming."[13] Against the grain of these readings, Plonowska Ziarek proposes the notion of a "radical female imaginary," one that inhabits the discontinuous temporality of history and exceeds the paradigm of visual representation. Here fluidity is no longer "subordinated to geometrism" and the drawing of fixed boundaries, like in the case of the mirror image, which Lacan famously defines in terms of "formal fixation" and "spatial captation."[14] For Plonowska Ziarek, this other imaginary takes shape through or around the "incompleteness and 'nonsuture' of form (expressed, for instance, in the image of the two lips)," in a space that is thoroughly permeated by time.[15] Excessive or, better, exceeding form is a matter of becoming—the indefinite transformation of a being that cannot be subsumed under the category of the subject: "Now woman is neither closed nor open.... Never this, then that, this and that.... But becoming the expansion that she is not, will never be at any moment, as a definable universe."[16]

I suspect that it is this neglected relation between fluidity, perception, and becoming that makes the Hannover sequence simultaneously conspicuous and elusive, pointing to a domain beyond "the threshold of the visible world"—that is, the mirror image according to Lacan. While Farocki does not explicitly pursue this line of inquiry, Jeff Wall does. In "Photography and Liquid Intelligence," Wall attends to photography's material and symbolic evacuation of water by putting forward the distinction between two kinds of intelligence, "liquid" and "dry."[17] Wall also calls the latter optical or "glassed-in" and identifies it with the optics and mechanics (lenses and shutter) at work in photography as an apparatus and an institution. On the other hand, he connects the former back to those production processes involving water ("washing, bleaching, dissolving") that, for him, lie at the "origin of techne" and now belong to photography's archaic history. This draining or binding of fluids is presented as simultaneously reductive and indispensable: "You certainly don't want any water in your camera, for example!" remarks Wall; water needs to be "controlled exactly" in both space and time for a picture to turn out at all.[18] What is lost in this displacing away from water has to do with photography's capacity to foster and even reconfigure memory, a capacity that Wall explicitly associates with liquid intelligence (and which Silverman would align with the look in her reading of *Bilder*).[19] In contrast, the dry part of the medium, in its privileging a "projectile or ballistic" understanding of vision, promotes a "cool," detached, and instrumental relationship to the perceptual world. We certainly find in *Bilder* several instantiations of this technological hubris; indeed, the film can be said to expose crucial phases or knots in the history of an intelligence that quantifies and calculates, turning "pictures into measurements" at the time of Albrecht Dürer, and now, in the age of computers, "measurements into pictures."[20] Indeed, for Wall, electronic and digital media extend and even exacerbate this problematic destiny of fluids, threatening to remove not only the actual use but also the recollection of water from the theory and practice of photography, a point that I will address directly in the chapter on Victor Burgin's digital projections.

However, if Wall believes that photography needs its dry, mechanical part, he is also adamant in observing that the latter can render the dynamics of fluidity. As an example, he offers his own picture *Milk* (1984), in which milk is seen spilling from its boxy container against the background of a brick wall. "The explosion of the milk from its container," he writes in the opening paragraph, "takes a shape which is not really describable or characterizable, but which provokes many associations. A natural form, with its unpredictable contours, is an expression of infinitesimal metamorphosis of quality."[21] I want to focus on this inaugural description as it does not oppose form to fluidity but, rather, points to a "kind of movement or form" that preserves and expresses it. Distinctive and yet without stable contours and quantifiable properties, this is a form that flows—a form that transforms itself in its apparent arrest. We encounter here the paradox of a fluid form (milk *as* it is spilling/being spilled) that emerges by means of an opposite movement, namely, "the mechanical character of the action of opening and closing the shutter—the substratum of instantaneity which persists in all photography."[22] It is by adjusting the shutter speed, which entails measuring time and light, that it is possible to register a qualitative transformation, the spilling of the milk in the instant in which it occurs. I will later contend that the thought of liquid intelligence cannot but disperse the fiction of the instant, even when it comes to photography, and that the time of the milk—a transparency in a light box—is of a richer, more enigmatic kind. At this juncture, what I want to emphasize is how the uncoupling of form and solidity runs through Wall's essay as the affirmation of a capacity for perception—for appearing and showing—that dissolves the divide between subject and object and the dry distance separating them.[23] If instrumental vision "has been separated to a great extent from the sense of immersion in the incalculable," which Wall associates with liquidity, there remains the promise of a return—of water, memory, and a futural past. This is what happens in Andrei Tarkovsky's *Solaris* (1972), where the scientists studying a mysterious oceanic planet find themselves studied in return, the planet sending back to them their own memories "in the form of hallucinations, perfect in every detail," so that "people from their pasts appear in the present and must be related to once again, maybe in a new way."[24] Memory arises here not from water as matter, like in Gaston Bachelard's *Water and Dreams,* but from the liquidity of form.[25]

The pre-Socratics had a name for this form that transforms itself, and it was rhythm, *rhuthmos*: a form or configuration that is "improvised, momentary, changeable," a "fluctuation" or "manner of flowing."[26] Émile Benveniste rediscovers this other sense of rhythm—or form—in ancient Ionian and Attic texts, and his research plays a pivotal role in my inquiry not only for its etymological virtuosity but also for its almost visionary character. In this chapter, I will turn to it as the attempt to reanimate a past of fragments where language and reality are imbricated otherwise, the blueprint of a project that belongs to a futural past. The lost world of contemplation to which *Bilder* refers and where the look is "itself implicated or 'tied up' with [its object]" is still a world of near-solids, objects and subjects. On the other hand, by attending to Benveniste's proposal and its implications for a psychoanalysis of rhythm, I begin to conceptualize rhuthmos as a form that is inseparable from the time of its appearance and, conjointly, a mode of being that undoes the divide of subject and object. With and beyond Philippe Lacoue-Labarthe's reinterpretation of Lacan, I will follow the traces of this radical imaginary as it emerges in Jean Vigo's *L'Atalante* (1934), a film that anticipates the mutation of postwar European cinema in its capacity to portray characters as *voyants*, seers of a vision that eludes their control.[27] More specifically, I will read its celebrated underwater sequence as a veritable dance of the atoms, a discreetly turbulent form and the image of form's forgotten liquidity. By virtue of montage and superimposition, the images of the two protagonists (Jean swimming, Juliette dancing) come together not as "two-in-one," the analogy of love or love as analogy, but as other-than-one, even less-than-one (as if one could multiply by subtracting), the image of a love beyond measure. Here rhuthmos emerges as a peculiar *form of life*, a mode of being with images that returns or persists only as an instance of becoming, the bearer of a temporality— that of the unconscious—that cannot be reduced to cadence or measured rhythm. Finally, I will show that this underwater dance does not belong to what Giorgio Agamben has called "nymphal life," the never fully realized union between subject and images (or nymphs). If anything, *L'Atalante* suggests that we need images in order to become other than subjects, to find ourselves anew as mutable configurations of being, forms of life that resist arrest and, with it, a definition of form that retains too much of the abstract formalism it is supposed to counter.

RHYTHM AS A MANNER OF FLOWING

In "The Notion of Rhythm in Its Linguistic Expression," Benveniste begins by questioning the commonly held conviction that the Greek term *rhuthmos*, having derived from *rhein* (to flow), was originally used to designate the regular movement of the waves. His precise and cogent research articulates itself in three main movements: first, he finds ample evidence that, in pre-Socratic philosophy and in lyric and tragic poetry, rhuthmos meant "configuration," "disposition," "form"; second, he shows that both the radical and the suffix (*-thmos*) concur to express the provisional character of this configuration, as it keenly distinguishes itself from the form defined by other terms (*skhema, morphe, eidos*, etc.); third, he identifies the crucial turn in the use of the term with Plato's adoption of rhuthmos to name the regulated movement of human bodies in a dance.[28] This last move will prove so successful that the earlier valence will become unavailable or, once retrieved, difficult to appreciate both linguistically and philosophically. In his study of Greek rhythm, Pierre Sauvanet stresses that not all scholars agree with Benveniste and himself advocates for the term's original polysemy, that is, an unresolved oscillation between the competing meanings of "holding" and "flowing."[29] Still, Sauvanet acknowledges that Plato's redefinition of rhuthmos constitutes a paramount reduction of the preexisting semantic field. Curiously, Benveniste's analysis is flat-out misread by thinkers as diverse as Deleuze and Guattari and Rodolphe Gasché and only succinctly addressed even by those, like Roland Barthes and Lacoue-Labarthe, who productively draw on its findings.[30] It is thus worth exploring it in some detail so as to avoid basic misapprehensions and further expand its reach.

Let us start, as Benveniste does, with the founders of atomism, Democritus and Leucippus, whose texts have reached us by means of Aristotle. According to Democritus, the differences between bodies are of three kinds: *rhuthmos* (rhythm), *diathige* (contact), and *trope* (turn), which Aristotle respectively equates to *skhema* (form), *taxis* (order), and *thesis* (position). However, by explaining *rhuthmos* with *skhema*, Aristotle at once transmits and inflects the original meaning of rhuthmos, that is, *form*: the form that atoms take, their configuration or arrangement. An example from Leucippus employing letters of the alphabet confirms that, at this early stage, rhuthmos names "the distinctive form, the characteristic arrangement of the parts into a whole" and also "the configuration of the signs of writing," an acceptation that will attract the attention of Martin Heidegger, Philippe Lacoue-Labarthe, and Jacques Derrida.[31] Benveniste also considers examples from lyric poetry and tragedy. In the former case, rhuthmos applies to the human character, its "attitude" or "disposition"; in the latter, the verb derived from it *(rhuthmizein)* means "to give form." In Sophocles's *Antigone*, for instance, it can be translated as "to picture, to localize": "Why do you picture the location of my grief?" replies Creon to the guard who wants to know whether his own voice is making the king suffer in his ears or in his soul.[32]

Having ascertained that *rhuthmos* signifies form, Benveniste proceeds to identify what sets it apart from the form named by the term *skhema*. He first underscores that the suffix *-(th)mos* modifies abstract words by expressing the *modality*, the manner in which something is accomplished: for instance, not "the act of dancing," but the "particular dance seen as it takes place." (A thinker of enunciation and deixis, Benveniste might have been particularly alert to such a modification.) Yet it is the radical that sets the term apart from its alleged synonyms. *Rhuthmos* does in fact derive from *rhein* (to flow), but not in the way it was assumed: far from designating regularity in movement, rhuthmos literally means "the particular manner of flowing." Here the difference between *rhuthmos* and *skhema* emerges as simultaneously subtle and irreducible. While *skhema* names "a fixed 'form,' realized and viewed in some way as an object," *rhuthmos* expresses

> the form in the instant that it is assumed by what is moving, mobile and fluid, the form of that which does not have organic consistency; it fits the pattern of a fluid element, of a letter arbitrarily shaped, of a robe which one arranges at one's will, of a particular state of character or mood. It is the form as improvised, momentary, changeable.

Form as rhuthmos is thoroughly marked by contingency and impermanence. In a world where all things are in flux, it can thus characterize the arrangement not only of what is "properly" liquid or fluid (water and air) but also of what we have come to regard as static or solid, for instance letters and garments. The originality of the term resides in having adopted a derivative of *rhein* to designate the "specific modality of the 'form,'" thus expressing the very tenets of a philosophy in which "*rhein* is the essential predication of nature and things."[33] Form as fluctuation appears as it is only in the process of becoming; it constitutes, to anticipate Lacoue-Labarthe's reading, a "form or figure broached necessarily by time."[34] It is in this sense that I interpret Benveniste's use of the expression "in the instant," as the affirmation not of pure instantaneity but of a simultaneity that is radical difference: "the same thing, then, in its difference [*en différence*]. *En diapheron heauto*," as Lacoue-Labarthe writes in an essay on Friedrich Hölderlin— "the One differing in itself."[35]

The break in the history of the term occurs when Plato adopts rhuthmos to define the regulated movement of human bodies in a dance: "this order in the movement has been given the name *rhythm*," he declares in the *Laws*, "while the order in the voice in which high and low combine is called *harmony*, and the union of the two is called the *choral art*."[36] Here rhuthmos's previous meaning is at once maintained and reduced: rhythm as arrangement becomes the controlled alternation of slow and rapid movements. A symmetry is established between the human body and the voice (and the latter's privileged relation to language and rationality), while both are assigned an order, a sense of order that in fact is what distinguishes human beings from animals. In other words, Plato still employs the term in the sense of "distinctive form, disposition, proportion," but now he mobilizes it to identify "the *form of movement*" that the dancing body produces in accordance with a criterion of numerical evaluation. Rhythm thus becomes "order in movement" *(kineseos taxis)*, a definition that resonates to this day despite the myriad modifications it has undergone. "The decisive circumstance is there," states Benveniste, "in the notion of a corporeal *rhuthmos* associated with *metron* and bound by the law of numbers: that 'form' is from then on determined by a 'measure' and numerically regulated." Far from constituting a mere technicality, this binding of form contributes to the dismantling of a philosophical tradition and the production of another: the transition from "*rhuthmos*, a spatial configuration," to "'rhythm,' a configuration of movements organized in time," coincides with nothing less than a turning away from "moving" as the becoming of all things.[37] Plato's rhythm, in its shift of emphasis from the realm of matter to that of the human and from space to chronological time, imposes itself as an attack (or defense) against Heraclitus's flux, thus partaking in a systematic regulation of the relationship between the sensible and the intelligible.[38]

There are profound ethical, and indeed political, implications to this shift—from rhuthmos as "the particular manner of flowing" to rhythm as "order in movement." It is worth noticing that the latter definition appears in the *Laws* as Plato explains that young people are reckless and unruly but that an exclusively human order comes to distinguish their movement: this order in movement is rhythm as it finds expression in the art of the chorus. In this respect, Sauvanet claims that, for Plato, aesthetic rhythm emerges as a means to an end, that is, as propaedeutic with respect to the ethical and political rhythm of the city-state; he also distinguishes Plato from Aristotle, as the latter attempts to introduce some distance between rhythm and meter (like in the case of oratory) and, concomitantly, gives plurality greater weight in his consideration of political life.[39] Yet there seems to be a more immediately ethical and political valence to the aesthetic of rhythm.

Lacoue-Labarthe gestures toward it in "The Echo of the Subject," where he underscores that, for Plato, what counts is "to get rid of all rhythmic variety and irregularity," to reduce multiplicity on behalf of simplicity and unity.[40] Thus, in the *Republic*, only those rhythms that "imitate the life (the style) of an ordered and virile man" can find a proper place in the city-state: now operating under the constraints of measure, rhythm at once reveals and gives form (in the sense of *skhema*, rigid form) to the ethos.[41] Lacoue-Labarthe exposes how this alliance between music and discourse works to curtail the power of mimesis: by interweaving the body and the voice in the tissue of measure, rhythm domesticates excess and dissimulation. Politics and identification meet at this very juncture.[42] On the other hand, in its lack of proper form, the rest is deemed arrhythmic and even mad, one might add, as in the distinction between "noble" and "mad" dance, the dance of the chorus and the trance of the Bacchantes, mania.[43]

Most important for the present inquiry, Lacoue-Labarthe positions Plato's *"theoretical decision"* with respect to rhythm in the context of the reduction that, in Western thought, the acoustic has undergone to the advantage of the visual. This reduction also applies to psychoanalysis and, without criticizing Sigmund Freud's "semiotics of verbal signifiers and visual forms" as directly as Derrida does, Lacoue-Labarthe proceeds to displace the alliance between *logos* and figure by working "with and against Lacan."[44] He is keenly aware that the endeavor to go back "from Narcissus to Echo"—from specular reflection to reverberation—requires more than shifting one's theoretical attention. In the tradition that spans from Plato to Lacan, the theoretical has constituted itself by mobilizing a "specular instrument"—that is, by joining the specular and the speculative in the production of consistency (a critique that Irigaray crucially articulates in relation to sexual difference).[45] Asking the question of rhythm precipitates a crisis at the heart of this hegemonic system to the very extent that the latter constituted itself also by reframing and reorienting the meaning of pre-Socratic rhuthmos. It leads the theoretician to theorize "at the limit of the theorizable."[46] Thus, in Lacoue-Labarthe's reading, even the Lacanian mirror image ends up multiplying from within or, better, discovering itself as already multiple: "the figure is never *one*," he writes; "there is no 'proper image' with which to identify totally, no essence of the imaginary." Lacoue-Labarthe pushes this economic crisis even further by affirming rhuthmos

FIGURE 1. *L'Atalante* (Jean Vigo, 1934): Jean looks for Juliette's image in the water of the canal.

as a crucial aspect in "the general differentiation of what is," a mode of articulation of the sensible in excess of specularity and, concomitantly, the trace of another mode of theoretical elaboration.[47]

MARINE LOVERS

What we see and hear: a mad, liquid, almost viscous dance; movement without order; a revolution of the elements. The brief underwater sequence in Jean Vigo's *L'Atalante* offers us not an image of disorderly rhythm but rhythm as disorderly image. I will point to this image by adopting the term rhuthmos in the attempt to foreground its being a self-differing form, the distinctive and yet ephemeral arrangement of a materiality that escapes the opposition of form and matter—a configuration of excessive matter, if you will. What I am trying to find, in the elusiveness of this other form

FIGURE 2. *L'Atalante* (Jean Vigo, 1934): Jean and Juliette's dance of the atoms.

(rhuthmos), is the potential for a life lived with and through images that cannot stop becoming or reinventing themselves; that return under the sign of wonder, *as if* for the first time, in an experience of repetition beyond repetition compulsion. In her reading of Irigaray, Plonowska Ziarek argues that a radical imaginary needs to destabilize the scopic economy of the mirror stage and that an ethics of sexual difference can only emerge once we reconceive female embodiment in terms not of "negative space" (like in the tradition that runs from Plato to Lacan) but of "disjunctive time." I would like to push this anti-identitarian politics of the image one step further and think of rhuthmos as an arrangement of the sensible that emerges in place of or next to the mirror image: not as another version of that "body in bits and pieces" that might precede the specular image as "first schema," but as a constellation of fragments that eludes any yearned-for or antagonized unity.[48] It is as rhuthmos that the image shows its ontological force,

FIGURE 3. *L'Atalante* (Jean Vigo, 1934): the image of the beloved is an echo.

emerging as a mode of being that, at least intermittently, de-creates and re-creates our experience across received divides of gender, sexuality, race, even species. I am reminded here of Jean Epstein's call for a cinema that, having freed itself from "egocentrism" and the "CGS zone of the human scale," can finally "encounter and reveal figures not yet hewn into classes and subclasses, provisionally without name (or definitely un-nameable), stupid and marvelous."[49] Abundant with differences, the perceptual domain engenders not self-identical forms but monstrous, scandalously surprising configurations.

I position Vigo's underwater sequence in the same force field as the slow-motion pillow fight scene in his *Zéro de conduite* (*Zero for Conduct*, 1933). In both cases, an element emerges as the medium of a revolution, an overturning of the physical and symbolic order of the body and its surroundings: air in the boarding school's dorm, water in the canal. If the children of *Zéro de conduite* find themselves under the punctual watch of the school authorities, the protagonists of *L'Atalante* are subjected to the more dispersed control of the canal network itself (only momentarily embodied by the company's manager), that is, by an economy of exchange that requires goods to circulate on time. Indeed, the canal and its flow of bound water is from the beginning more than mere background: for the small colony of *L'Atalante*, life is first and foremost life on "L'Atalante," the river barge. It is within the enclosure of the barge, a sort of fluvial heterotopia, that the characters tacitly partake in an experiment—living together and yet each according to their own rhythm. I borrow the terms of this ethical and political experiment from Roland Barthes, who turns to the notion of rhuthmos to explore "idiorrhythmy" as the idiosyncratic form of a living together "at a distance," a spatial and temporal arrangement in which fantasy plays a key role. For Barthes, this other mode of life always holds "a negative relationship to power": it proves incompatible with any strong architecture of power (large communes, phalansteries, convents, etc.) and instead finds itself closer to the *diaita* (diet, lifestyle) of early monastic clusters, which operated "outside a superior's control."[50] In this context, I am interested in connecting Barthes's notion of idiorrhythmy as a form that directly pertains to life to the emergence of eccentric images of self and other—what one might call an *eccentric life of images*.

On the barge, along with countless cats, we find four people: Jean, the young captain and Juliette's newly wedded husband; old Père Jules, the first mate, whose tattooed body amounts to a true cabinet of curiosities, like his sleeping quarters; the cabin boy, an accordion player; and Juliette, a young woman from the country and Jean's newly wedded bride, whose desire for the distant sounds and images of the city will soon clash with the restrictions of the barge. Life onboard unfolds according to a routine of basic chores, domestic and otherwise, which is interrupted only by extemporaneous interactions between Juliette and Père Jules and infrequent visits offshore. That these diversions provoke Jean's jealousy is to be attributed less to a direct rivalry between male opponents than to the fact that both Père Jules and the young street peddler, whom they meet while out on the town, open up for Juliette a world of diffuse desire: queer, polymorphous, inseparable from some kind of image or sound technology.[51] In truth, Juliette is fascinated by all sorts of prostheses of the body, including the (mirror) image as it might appear in a body of water. "Don't you know you can see your beloved's face in the water?" she says to Jean sometime after the wedding. Perhaps she is registering that the beloved's image is but an idealized image of the self, a "looking glass," as Virginia Wolf would specifically say of women's bodies and their "magic and delicious power of reflecting the figure of man at twice its natural size"; perhaps she is intuiting something else, like a haphazard play of reflections, indifferent to gender hierarchies.[52] She herself has been prey to these visions: "When I was little, I saw things like that," she explains. "And last year, I saw your image in the water. That's why I first recognized you when you first came to the house." Anyway, Jean responds to her folk anecdote by dismissively placing his face first into a basin, then in the canal itself, and failing to see anything. Now, after an indeterminate period of cohabitation, they find themselves apart: Juliette has ventured into the city without informing him, and Jean, husband and captain, has taken revenge by leaving her ashore, stranded. In the aftermath of this decision, he falls into a prolonged state of melancholia and it is from the depth of this mood that he abruptly dives overboard, in search of Juliette's image.

In a scene of surreal beauty, Jean is shown swimming underwater, his eyes wide open and his mouth tightened. The waltz that Père Jules's phonograph is playing onboard remains audible, transforming his movements into a strange dance. While the camera remains still, we see Jean swimming toward us, performing a somersault, and then swimming back and forth, his body always exceeding the borders of the frame. We can almost feel the density of the water, the pressure it exercises on the swimmer, and what looks like a swarm of air bubbles reminds us of the animality of breathing. It is as if we were encountering some marine creature, caught in the murkiness of the canal; or as if, like in the case of Anita Conti's photographs of life at sea, we were witnessing the "discovery of a point-of-view closer to the fish than to the fisherman"; or as if, like in Epstein's essay, the human eye underwent an ever-twisting mutation by virtue of its association with the camera.[53] Finally, the image of Juliette appears, almost like a fairytale vision. The use of the vibraphone produces an effect that is at once metallic and dreamy, like an acoustic shimmering that we cannot quite locate.[54] Meanwhile, the camera does not move, nor does the editing employ an eye-line match to connect the look of the two lovers. Instead, Juliette and

Jean are superimposed in a dance that brings them together but does not coordinate their movements according to an external parameter. At first, Juliette becomes visible as a miniature figure, in her white wedding gown, as she slowly turns towards us. Then her image disappears, and we see only Jean's face, until a dissolve makes Juliette's face appear against a black background, a strong wind discomposing her hair. She smiles and looks elusively somewhere off-screen, her countenance now endowed with a kind of watery luminosity. A final dissolve brings Jean's face back into view and makes Juliette fade away.

The beauty of the sequence is one of discontinuity, of small internal discordances. Images are not made to fit one another in size or tempo; they are even enveloped in different elements (water in Jean's case, air in Juliette's). Indeed, it is as if they remain slightly unglued, disjointed in their very encounter. Meanwhile, Jean and Juliette are given the chance to partake in what Barthes would call an "erotics of distance."[55] At once ephemeral and intricate, this dance does not encompass the image of the beloved (whether we take the latter to be Juliette or, in a gesture of reciprocity, Jean); it does not hold it in view as its object. Rather, the image of the beloved *is* this dance. Here the narcissism of the body proper dissolves into a blurring configuration, a novel arrangement of matter. Instead of the specular image, we find the reverberation or "echo" of the image, radiant and yet not rigidly formalized. Jean and Juliette's encounter finds itself at a point of maximum divergence from the one occurring twice between Scottie and Madeleine/Judy in Alfred Hitchcock's *Vertigo* (1958): first at the restaurant, when Madeleine's profile acquires the brilliance of a jewel while remaining fixed, held in check as an object by Scottie's look; then when Scottie, after a yearlong crisis of melancholia, resumes his wanderings through San Francisco and sees the beloved again, and again sees her only as a profile, a silhouette, a cut-out figure. That, in both instances, Madeleine/Judy does not, indeed cannot, reciprocate Scottie's look is less important than the fact that these two phases (looking and being looked at) would be given in succession, in a sort of cadenced alternation. By contrast, Jean and Juliette find each other in the simultaneity of a configuration that cannot stop becoming other than itself. This is more than saying that the look encounters a transitory form, or that it reanimates the fixed form it encounters. Rather, here the look itself is so imbricated in the materiality of things that it becomes but one of its many elusive configurations *(rhuthmoi)*.

The mood of the encounters, too, is markedly different. In *Vertigo,* the thrill of the perfect form sends the detective back into the city, that is, keeps people and things in circulation. In *L'Atalante,* wonder, even a kind of stupor, occurs in place of jubilation, restrained or otherwise, and it will take Père Jules's ingenuity and the marvels of recorded sound to reunite the lovers. One might surmise that among Père Jules's motives for tracking down Juliette and rescuing Jean from his apathy and, later, deep longing was also the need to restore the efficiency of the barge's commercial schedule. In fact, what rhuthmos ultimately disrupts is the very principle of economy, the alliance of form and value as it imposes itself at the psychic and social levels, pointing instead, to borrow again from Irigaray's critique, "towards what cannot be defined, enumerated, formulated, formalized."[56] Such a crisis poses a profound challenge not to the subject's economy but, rather, to the economy that makes it possible to speak of a subject, including the allegedly antieconomic workings of the death drive. In this respect, it would be hard to ignore the role that repetition compulsion plays in *Vertigo,* and not only in the case of Scottie's obsessional neurosis. It is also more than a coincidence that Lacoue-Labarthe attends to rhythm while investigating the connection between autobiography and musical obsession in Theodor Reik's oeuvre. There he finds the traces of an internal "erosion," a wearing away of the subject's economy as the latter discovers himself always oscillating between "*at least* two figures (or a figure that is *at least* double)": for instance, "between the artist and the scientist, between Mahler and Abraham, between Freud and Freud."[57] Is Jean another example of this "subject in 'desistance'"? A subject who "de-constitutes" himself while looking for an impossible image? In this case, Jean and Juliette's liquid dance would surface only as a longed-for break from repetition compulsion, a temporary suspension of its demonic force; a sort of benevolent counterpart to Scottie's vision of Judy, as the latter finally reappears as Madelaine in the motel room's green, foggy light. If I am hesitant to pursue this line of interpretation, it is because I sense that something more radical is at play in this dance, something that could undermine the very conditions under which repetition compulsion has been theorized. Lacoue-Labarthe, too, entertains this possibility as he attempts to reach beyond Reik by disengaging the question of rhythm from that of music—that is, by disentangling it "from a problematic that is exclusively one of temporal repetition, energetic alternance, pulsation and interruption, cadence and measure."[58] He turns to rhuthmos and its excess with respect to metrics at this very juncture, in the endeavor to do what Reik could not: exposing and pushing beyond the limits of Freud's theorization of the death drive.

However, "The Echo of the Subject" does not end with this opening toward the impossibility of closure. As soon as he reaches *beyond* the "double bind" of Reik's version of narcissism, Lacoue-Labarthe also retreats. "Perhaps it is impossible to get beyond the closure of narcissism," he intimates, proposing that we regard the "maternal voice" as the inescapable origin of this destiny.[59] He then quotes two texts: an essay by psychoanalyst Georg Groddeck on the agreement between the regular rhythms of the mother and child's heartbeats during the pregnancy; and a poem by Wallace Stevens on "children and old men and philosophers" being haunted by the maternal voice. At the risk of underplaying the challenge that music and poetry have posed for the problematic of the unconscious, I will say that the limit encountered in this case strikes me as eminently sociosymbolic. It is as if, after upsetting the Lacanian distinction between the imaginary and the symbolic, Lacoue-Labarthe could not avoid repeating, albeit at a different level, what he has called Reik's productive failure, getting caught himself in a web of filiations that he cannot quite unravel. It is Derrida who directs our attention to the thickness of this web when he highlights Lacoue-Labarthe's theoretical courage in scattering the very paradigm of identification by multiplying its figures. This applies not only to Reik but also to Lacoue-Labarthe himself, who, according to Derrida, would be oscillating between "Mahler, von Buhlow and Beethoven, Reik, Abraham, and Freud . . . But also Heidegger and Lacan, Rousseau, Hegel, Nietzsche, and Girard. And Groddeck and Thomas Mann and Leucippus. And Wallace Stevens." Derrida aptly calls it "a constant multiplication of filiations, denials of filiation or paternity."[60] It is here, in this claustrophobic archival site, that I find the closure that Lacoue-Labarthe ends up attributing to the maternal.

Rhuthmos as vibrating form or fluctuation does not ensue from the multiplication of the imago. Rather, as Lacoue-Labarthe suggests while being himself captured in this play of duplications, "the imago has no fixity or proper being."[61] If it were a matter of external proliferation or internal splitting of the one, then rhuthmos would still serve the reasons of homology or, in Irigaray's terminology, "hommology."[62] Derrida senses this risk when he writes, "The double bind as such is still too linked to opposition, contradiction, dialectic . . . it still belongs to *that kind* of undecidable that derives from calculation and from a nervous dialectical contradiction." However, by emphasizing the percussive, indeed *compulsive* aspects of rhythm as spacing, and attending to rhuthmos only in its valence as signature or imprint, Derrida, too, will only go so far in moving beyond the double bind of "the knot and the caesura."[63] Indeed, he will not even go as far as Lacoue-Labarthe does in his recuperation of rhuthmos as a mode of differentiation that, while "bearing a relation to archi-écriture," also exceeds its logic of inscription.[64] That is, Lacoue-Labarthe reaches beyond *arche-writing* as tracing until the turbulence that his move engenders needs to be channeled "back" into the acoustics of the maternal body, which in this version happens to be regulated by a beat. What he discovers in the meantime is that the imago is not an object to begin with or, rather, that it is one only for what Irigaray calls a "mechanics of near-solids," a theory and practice of psychoanalysis that has decided to give desire an *object*. In a libidinal economy of near-solids (objects and subjects), albeit of the most sophisticated kind, one ought to account for and regulate what does not fit, what threatens to overflow. "Thus certain properties of the 'vital,'" writes Irigaray, "have been deadened into the 'constancy' required to give it form," which is what the death drive might also be said to do.[65] Ultimately, by linking maternal closure to repetition compulsion, Lacoue-Labarthe maintains a certain libidinal economy in movement *and* in place: in place by virtue of a movement that follows a beat, a cadence (*fort-da*) that, it is worth remembering, was first registered as such in a domestic setting.[66]

RHUTHMOS AS A FORM OF LIFE

There is nothing womb-like or tomb-like in the water of *L'Atalante*, certainly not in the lovers' dance sequence. There is also no erotic complementarity between Jean and Juliette as their figures float together at a distance, arranged in the space and time of a slightly dissonant tune, each moving in their own medium. I want to emphasize this disjunction against the temptation to consider the underwater dance as an episode in that "life of images" which Giorgio Agamben seals under the rubric of "nymphs." In fact, the latter emerges as contained, even blocked within a fragmentary and yet self-enclosed lineage, one that showcases Bill Viola, Domenichino, Aby Warburg, Henry Darger, Walter Benjamin, Paracelsus, and Boccaccio as *subjects* and nymphs as object-like images. According to Agamben, this eclectic genealogy indicates that "the history of the ambiguous relation between men and nymphs is the history of the difficult relation between man and his images."[67] On the other hand, it is my contention that this history can establish itself as such only on the basis of a preliminary evacuation of fluidity—which is also an evacuation of time as becoming—from the texture of the image. In Agamben's conceptualization of the image (cinematographic and otherwise), what follows this unacknowledged exclusion is a "reintroduction" of time through movement and, conjointly, a gendering of the relation between the image and the subject who is charged with the task of releasing its temporality. This narrative of release is to be traced back to a privileging of arrest over flow, movement over time, that informs not only Agamben's account of nymphal life but also his very notion of *form-of-life*. After *L'Atalante*, I will maintain that rhuthmos as fluctuation pertains to another life of images and, indeed, emerges as a form of life to the very extent that it evades the arrest that has marked the thought of difference (sexual and otherwise).

Let me focus on the incipit of this genealogy of arrest as it takes shape in "Nymphs." Agamben turns to Domenichino's fifteenth-century treatise on dance in response to the question, "How can an image charge itself with time?" which he was prompted to formulate after seeing Bill Viola's videos and realizing that they "insert not the images in time but time in the images." As such, the question seems to imply that an image can be "without" time, but perhaps Agamben is addressing a historical depletion, the loss of time that has befallen the image in our society of the spectacle, and he reserves the term *time* for a much rarer kind of temporality. After all, he clearly states that "the real paradigm of life in the modern era is not movement but time."[68] Yet the recovery of Domenichino's "dance through phantasmata," which pivots on moments of arrest, points to a conceptualization of the image that is still much indebted to movement or, more precisely, to what Deleuze names "the subordination of time to movement."[69]

It might not be coincidental that, in "Notes on Gesture" and the essay on Guy Debord's films, Agamben references only Deleuze's movement-image, as if his proposal for an "imageless" cinema could function in lieu of a philosophy of the time-image. Except that it does not. The rediscovery of gesture through the protocinematic work of Eadweard Muybridge goes hand in hand with the recuperation of dance through Domenichino: in both cases, what is made visible is not time but a certain measurable articulation of movement through time. For instance, Domenichino's "'phantasm' (*fantasma*)" coincides with "a sudden arrest between two movements that virtually contracts within its internal tension the measure and the memory of the entire choreographic series."[70] Agamben is careful in pointing out that this interruption is not absolute but, rather, "simultaneously charged with memory and dynamic energy" and thus inherently open to reprise. But he has no qualms about a dance that is conceived as a sequential ordering of movement (which is not far from Plato's conception of rhythm in choral art), a choreographic arrangement through which time is made visible in space according to a criterion of numerical evaluation. Unlike Deleuze, what Agamben seems to sidestep is the question that Henri Bergson asks of duration: "How would it appear to a consciousness which desired only to see it without measuring it, which would then grasp it without stopping it?"[71] As a result, time can appear only in its suspension, a halting that is abrupt and yet written in beforehand. Warburg's *pathos formulae*, cinema's film stills, and Domenichino's phantasms are all charged with time to the extent that they preserve the trace of the *order* of movement in time that they bring to a stop—almost but not quite, so that they can be reanimated once again. (Something feels puppetlike in this picture, and I cannot help thinking of Casanova's dance with the beautiful automaton in Federico Fellini's *Casanova* [1976]; Barthes, who was intensely touched by it, writes of discovering, in this scene as in photography, the "pangs of love."[72] I do too. It is after all a matter of love, but this does not make it any less ambiguous.)

In Agamben's "Nymphs," time is outside—in the image or gesture— and not in the interiority of the subject, but it still requires a subject in order to be released. Such a subject is ostensibly neutral, apart from the fact that, once again, it is not. Nowhere is this more evident than in the staging of the amorous encounter between "men and nymphs." In Paracelsus, whose work will influence Warburg, nymphs are the "elemental spirits" connected to water, "creatures" that do not possess a soul but can obtain one "if they enter into sexual union with a man and generate a child with him."[73] For Agamben, in their incomplete (feminine) nature, nymphs are thus *images* par excellence; the cipher of the split between the corporeal and the incorporeal that haunts the human being; the mark of a "purely historical life." However, while emerging as "the ideal archetype of every separation of man from himself," nymphs do not stand on equal terms with him, and the same can be said of images: "in order to be truly alive, images, like Paracelsus's elemental spirits, need a subject to unite with them."[74] In other words, for the pause or arrest to coincide with the emergence of another temporality (even a potentially revolutionary one, as in the case of Agamben's reading of Benjamin), a subject is needed and this subject is male. One might surmise that a subject was already needed to bring these images to a standstill or, rather, that a subject emerged in the very performance of a gesture (halting) that would then be posited as something that is "endured" rather than produced or acted out.[75] If Agamben's nymphal world as well as his cinema of the gesture bear the traces of a telos it is in this positing of a metamorphosis that occurs "in fits and starts," so to speak: "Which would imply one figure taking over—from—the previous figure and prescribing the next: *one* form arrested, therefore, and becoming *another*. Which happens only in the imaginary of the (male) subject."[76] In the essay on Debord, this fantasy of interruption is called "power of stoppage."[77]

It is worth noticing that, in "Toward a Modal Ontology," Agamben addresses the etymology of rhuthmos, and it is here that a selective misreading of Benveniste, like a blind spot in the philosopher's erudition, reveals a form that is still bound to and by measure. If "being as being" is a being that cannot be separated from its "mode," Agamben reminds us, "one of the fundamental meanings of 'mode' is in fact the musical one of rhythm, just modulation."[78] It is in this context that he introduces Benveniste's distinction between *rhuthmos* and *schema,* referring then to Plato as the one who "applies the term to the ordered movements of the body." However, he detects no twist in Plato's intervention, a *"theoretical decision,"* as Lacoue-Labarthe calls it, that in fact entails a shift from what is moving in a world where all things are in flux to the ordered sphere of human movement.[79]

Moreover, while Benveniste makes clear that rhuthmos was not a musical category, Agamben takes it as a pretext for speaking of the "music of being" and describing being as "a substance [that] 'modulates' itself and beats out its rhythm . . . in the modes." For Agamben, "mode expresses this 'rhythmic' and not 'schematic' nature of being," and yet this rhythm remains connected to measure: the measure not only of the beat ("beating out") but also of the proper ("just measure," "just modulation").[80] I will notice that this smoothing over of the break between the pre-Socratics and Plato works in accord with the model of dance proposed in "Nymphs" and the fantasy of a flux that needs interruption in order to express the sheer potential of the gesture. One might find in the latter the traces of Werner Jaeger's interpretation of rhuthmos, which will influence Heidegger's thought of rhythm as "rest" and interfere with the reception of Benveniste.[81] In *Paideia*, Werner Jaeger insists on the univocal meaning of rhuthmos as a fixed form or pattern for which the term *skhema* constitutes an adequate translation. Without equivocation, rhythm is "that which imposes bonds on movement and confines the flux of things." The opposition between flow and form finds here its most extreme formulation: "the original conception which lies beneath the Greek discovery of rhythm in music and dancing is not *flow* but *pause*, the steady limitation of movement."[82] Not only in music and dance but also in the case of "a building or a statue," rhuthmos is what binds or enchains the flux of things: the grip, the grasp, the capture. The political implication of this stance should be noted: at the end of his defense of rhythm as interruption, Jaeger underlines the natural link existing between order in the character of man and order in the city-state; rhythm operates at this juncture, or, rather, it constitutes its very joint.

Aside from issues of etymological consistency, this crossing of Heraclitus and Plato, Benveniste and Jaeger concurs to give form, if you will, to a thought of potentiality that revolves around arrest: "the temporality of mode," writes Agamben, "is not actuality: it is, in present existence or in the actual, the gap that impedes their coinciding with themselves—the operative time in which the flux of being *pulsates and stops*, takes itself up and repeats itself and, in this way, modulates itself in a rhythm."[83] If the "non-coincidence of the moment with itself," the present's own internal discrepancy, seems to allow for an incredible leeway, it does so in a covertly regulated manner, finding the principle of this regulation in rhuthmos as a form that justly beats out the substance of being. But beating out does not account for all forms of modulation, implementing instead a reduction of the sensible that emerges with a vengeance in the choreography of nymphal love. Indeed, such a simplification betrays a dependency on that abstract formalism that makes it possible to speak of severing life from its form: if the production of bare life is always an "aftereffect," it is nonetheless foreshadowed in a definition of form that still defers to a principle of equivalence.[84] It also perpetually binds resistance to potentiality as impotentiality, to Bartleby's "I prefer not to." In "Feminine 'I can,'" Plonowska Ziarek turns to Anna Akhmatova's "I can" as the figure of another potentiality, that of a community in which the "impossible" character of sexual difference becomes the springboard for the creation of new forms of life through political praxis.[85] While I am sympathetic to the reasons behind this reassessment, here I propose that we step back and question Agamben's notion of potentiality in light of his conceptualization of rhythm, which is nothing less than the form that is at stake in form-of-life as "a life that can never be separated from its form."[86] To the extent that rhythm conforms to the law of alternation between fast and slow, arrest and reprise, like in Domenichino's dance through phantasmata, being as being is still covertly modulated in accordance to an external measure and resistance can only be envisioned as de-creation—that is, deactivation of what has been implicitly posited as an order. In fact, there is more to modern cinema than the play of repetition and stoppage that Agamben finds in the films of Guy Debord.

In excess of this fantasy, *L'Atalante*'s underwater sequence points us in the direction of another kind of intermittence, a discontinuity and unpredictability of form that rhuthmos as fluctuation can help us better articulate. Let me state this more directly: what I propose is that, rather than thinking of rhuthmos as unresolved interruption, we reconceive of interruption—the jolts, the summersaults, the standstills of montage—as rhuthmos, a vibration that defies the memory of the measure. This vibration might remind us of Benjamin's "trembling" projections in the first version of "What Is the Epic Theatre?" and in fact it shares with them a capacity for astonishment that is not the opposite of critique but its lining.[87] And yet, in the waters of *L'Atalante*, there is no "cliff from whose heights one looks down into the stream of things."[88] Neither gradual nor teleological, the temporality of rhuthmos also exceeds the metrics of the ebb and flow, never allowing us to rest and never draining us of energy—that is, never fully exhausting our potential to be otherwise. Unlike Agamben's gesture, whose power of interruption applies not only to action but also to "being as being," rhuthmos brings about not only the deactivation of an apparatus of capture (narrative cinema, in our case) but also the fleeting emergence of new forms of life. Indeed, rhuthmos affirms itself as a form of life. After Barthes and beyond Agamben, I adopt the expression to touch on a mode of living of the image—of images among themselves—that unfolds beyond the divide of subject and object and its distilled tempos. Underwater and elsewhere, what affirms itself as singular is the way images come together in a configuration that does not bind them—or, to borrow again from Barthes, what is singular is the idiorrhythmic cluster, the constellation beyond measure. It is also in this sense that cinema's rediscovery of the echo of water in technology might constitute one of its most relevant political functions.

2. Labor

MONTAGE, AFTER HOUSEWORK

"The cinema, in documentary and other forms, has rarely filmed work," states Jean-Louis Comolli at the beginning of an article translated by Annette Michelson.[1] He continues by referencing cinema's inaugural film, *La sortie de l'usine Lumière à Lyon* (*Employees Leaving the Lumière Factory*, 1895), in which factory workers exit the space of production to enter that of consumption, as a prescient example of this neglect; he then mentions Fritz Lang's *Metropolis* (1927) and Charlie Chaplin's *Modern Times* (1936) as qualified exceptions, so that one might suspect that, for him, industrial labor stands for labor tout court. Later references to his own films and Claire Simon's *Coûte que coûte* (*At All Costs*, 1995) will expand the sphere of production to include administrative and entrepreneurial work. Yet it is Dziga Vertov's Человек с кино-аппаратом (*Man with a Movie Camera*, 1929) that sets the stage for exploring the "machinic kinship of cinema and the world of labor, mechanized or otherwise," that is, for pursuing the desire to film the body at work where the machines of the visible and the visibility of machines share the same force field.[2] Harun Farocki seems to confirm cinema's century-long desertion of labor in a text commenting on his own film essay, *Arbeiter verlassen die Fabrik* (*Workers Leaving the Factory*, 1995), which opens with the Lumière sequence and is entirely composed of clips taken from newsreels, fiction films, and documentaries: "Films about work or workers have not become one of the main genres," he writes, "and the space in front of the factory has remained on the sidelines. Most narrative films take place in that part of life where work has been left behind."[3] If cinema returns to this first exodus throughout the twentieth century, Farocki suggests, it is in the attempt to master what it could not stop: the turning of workers into spectators of an apparatus that eludes their material and symbolic control. Ultimately, for Farocki as for Comolli, the line separating the factory from its outside via the chronotope of the gate coincides with the line keeping work and life apart and, by and large, only one of these domains—life before or after work—has commanded cinema's attention.[4]

And then it was already too late. With the advent of post-Fordism and the spreading of work into the more generalized texture of life, it became too late to film labor, at least the kind of labor that had distinguished modernity and its reshaping of space and time. So when Farocki received the commission for *Contre-chante* (*Counter-Music*, 2004) from the city of Lille, a former textile manufacturing stronghold and now a transportation hub and aspiring "new media center," he reflected on the impossibility of remaking the great 1920s city films. Regarding an actual remake, Thomas Schadt's *Berlin: Sinfonie einer Großstadt* (*Berlin: Symphony of a City*, 2002), he dryly observes that "it is still possible today to show people on their way to work streaming out of the city's transport system, even if large-scale industries have largely disappeared from the city—and today's melodies do not emanate from the *rhythm* of the machines."[5] Keenly aware of the transformations brought about by immaterial forms of labor, he adds, "The introduction of flexi time, the abstract complexity of most working processes and decreasing residential density—all of this robs the images created after Ruttmann of their energy."[6] How, then, can one portray a city that no longer functions according to the symphonic rhythms of industrial production? To start with, in addition to newly filmed footage, Farocki assembles different kinds of images: surveillance footage, digital graphs and diagrams, and what he dubs "operational" images—images meant not for the human eye but for an algorithmic software. He also interweaves clips from the opening of *Man with a Movie Camera*, a treatise on rhythm in its own right, but not without a crucial qualification. "For Dziga Vertov," says a title in *Counter-Music*, "the day begins with the production of images," whereas "for us, the day begins with their reproduction." Meanwhile, images of the cameraman's dynamic entry into the city space at dawn and the awakening of the city itself is contrasted with prerecorded images of dopey sleepers in a medical laboratory.

But was it always too early or too late? Is there an alternative to a history of film labor that, despite a touch of melodramatic temporality, still keeps past and future in line? In this chapter, I propose that we sketch a counter-genealogy of the relation between labor, montage, and rhythm by looking at a kind of labor that has indeed found visibility, if not in all cinema at least in Italian Neorealism and films that have emerged in its wake. I refer here to domestic labor. Apparently, it has not been too difficult to ignore or forget the recurring visibility of this invisible kind of labor, which in fact was long relegated outside the sphere of production proper.[7] Many remember the factory sequence in Roberto Rossellini's *Europa '51* (*Europe '51*, 1952) or at least what Ingrid Bergman later says about her experience there: "I thought I was seeing convicts." Gilles Deleuze writes about it in *Cinema 2* and, in "Postscript on the Societies of Control," quotes Bergman while remarking that the prison has provided the "analogical model" for the enclosures typical of the disciplinary societies (family, school, factory, among others).[8] As late as 2000, Harun Farocki uses the phrase as the title for a piece on prison surveillance, *Ich glaubte Gefangene zu sehen* (*I Thought I Was Seeing Convicts*). Yet few remember that Bergman sets foot in the factory because she is filling in for the character played by Giulietta Masina, a single mother of six whom she meets while visiting a desolate neighborhood on the outskirts of Rome. The scenes showing their unlikely encounter, which takes place in a shack at the edge of a new housing project, immediately precede the factory sequence and stand out as some of the finest depictions of housework in postwar cinema. Caught between Italy's industrial future and its premodern past, domestic labor temporarily subverts the constraints of the prison model to which factory labor will conform. In this respect, Masina's eccentric style stands out less as a diegetic ruse than as the index of an alternative mode of life: for instance, when she explains that, of her six children, three are her own, while three she has "picked up," informally taken under her care; or when she declines, in fact refuses, to show up at the factory on her first day because she had already planned to meet a boyfriend from out of town. But the prolonged visibility accorded here to mundane chores (doing the laundry, feeding and washing the children) is not an exception in neorealist cinema. As Cesare Casarino notes in "Images for Housework," depictions of domestic labor abound in the very films that are considered foundational to cinema's postwar renewal, from Luchino Visconti's *Ossessione* (*Obsession*, 1943) and *La terra trema* (*The Earth Trembles*, 1948) to Vittorio De Sica's *Ladri di biciclette* (*Bicycle Thieves*, 1948) and *Umberto D.* (1952). Most important, their sustained engagement with duration plays a crucial and yet neglected role in the transition from the movement-image to the time-image that marks Deleuze's philosophy of cinema and that Casarino reinterprets in light of the distinction between representation and expression.[9]

I began experimenting with the contours of this other genealogy of film and labor in my video essay *Philosophy in the Kitchen* (2014), which I composed as a response to both Casarino's article and Farocki's *Workers Leaving the Factory*.[10] There I gleaned, reframed, and edited side-by-side images of housework from mostly European cinema, including not only neorealist films but also films produced much later, such as Chantal Akerman's *Jeanne Dielman, 23, quai du Commerce, 1080 Bruxelles* (1975), Rainer W. Fassbinder's *Angst essen Seele auf* (*Ali: Fear Eats the Soul*, 1974), Marco Ferreri's *Dillinger è morto* (*Dillinger Is Dead*, 1969), Jean-Luc Godard's *Deux ou trois choses que je se sais d'elle* (*Two or Three Things I Know about Her*, 1967), Alexander Kluge's *Gelegenheitsarbeit einer Sklavin* (*Part-Time Work of a Domestic Slave*, 1973), Ettore Scola's *Una giornata particolare* (*A Special Day*, 1977), and Ousmane Sembène's *La Noire de . . .* (*Black Girl*, 1966). If I quote them in alphabetical order, it is to dispel the expectation that the counter-genealogy I am interested in tracing might depend on chronology or hold a classificatory purpose. While research was extensive, I was not attempting to document how visible this invisible kind of work had been or demonstrating neorealism's ripple effect. Rather, I was invested in producing a sort of undisciplined choreography of labor. My wish was to bring images together across time and let them endure "at the same time," as if they existed in a zone of intermittent and dispersed simultaneity. The logic of this necessarily incomplete assemblage, one that mobilizes housework in place of metallurgy as a principle of archival invention, remains operative in the present chapter.[11] In her work on duration and the everyday in European cinema, Ivone Margulies compares and contrasts renowned kitchen scenes from *Umberto D., Jeanne Dielman*, and *Two or Three Things I Know about Her* in order to expose their divergence, pointing to the essentialist character of Neorealism and opposing, within anti-essentialist cinema, Akerman's "aesthetics of homogeneity" to Godard's "aesthetics of heterogeneity."[12] What distinguishes my approach is not that I disagree with her assessment of Neorealism (even if I do) but the fact that I first look for the difference that exists in the image itself—in the image as other-than-itself—so as to follow its openness to becoming. In this sense, my counter-genealogy runs along anti-genealogical lines, fissured and convoluted, and remains reluctant to tidy up, to match ends with means, that is, to do dutiful housework.

One would be pressed to find images of housework proper in Farocki's *Counter-Music*. Yet, the city it portrays has been transformed by the so-called "feminization" of labor, and its rhythms are now those of an economy marked by virtually uninterrupted forms of production.[13] This economy finds in domestic labor and the mobilization of sexual difference an unwilling model: well before other forms of labor in our global system erased the line between work and life, housework was always that with which we are never done. In "Rules for the Incommensurable," Christian Marazzi points out that, in its utter porosity, the "live labor" typical of the domestic sphere has become central to the post-Fordist regime, like in the case of the information economy. However, where "machinery (constant capital) is less important than personal work," there emerges a crisis in the measure of value that radically upsets the capacity to convert quality into quantity.[14] How does one adequately calculate what goes into always knowing (as women do) where the "'proper place for the socks'" is and thus effortlessly putting them "'where they belong'"? Behind women's habitual gestures one finds centuries of gendered role distribution and a lifelong journey of unpaid training, so that the greater efficiency, the "intensity" with which they perform mundane tasks, remains impossible to quantify. The questions of sexual equality cannot be treated in a purely juridical fashion to the extent that the law relies on a measuring unit, while the complexity of domestic labor calls for a reassessment of the very "*nature* of the measuring device." Marazzi speaks here of the "incommensurable" as the subjective and historical density of live labor, "a disparity in experience that escapes any reduction to units of measure, to units applied to qualitatively heterogeneous quantities of concrete labor."[15] What economic science has expunged from its disciplinary field, and what needs to be recovered through a political analysis, is the contradiction that marks the very attempt to reduce quality to quantity, that is, to deal formally with a surplus that is the result of asymmetric power relations. Marazzi suggests that, while the notion of incommensurability has been haunting economics since Adam Smith, it has gained traction in the context of an economy where communicative kinds of labor have dramatically increased and where relational dynamics and hence language have become primary sites of both exploitation and struggle.

What is key for me is that this excess, this intractability of labor time with respect to measure, not to speak of language's productive role, all were already being addressed by Italian feminists in the 1970s (for instance, through the provocation of the Salario al Lavoro Domestico, or Wages for Housework, movement) and, before then, acquiring visibility in neorealist cinema.[16] The expression "labor of the head and heart," which Antonio Negri and Michael Hardt adopt in lieu of "immaterial labor," would hardly resonate as it deserves outside of this history of engagement with the practice of housework and the emphasis placed on metonymy by feminist philosophers like Luce Irigaray and Luisa Muraro.[17] Similarly, the distinction between "outside measure" and "beyond measure," the immeasurable and the virtual, which Hardt and Negri draw at the end of *Empire*, gains new complexity in light of the challenge that domestic labor has been posing to measure far ahead of the information economy.[18] In fact, the vicissitudes of housework suggest that evading rigid measuring does not entail evading control or even confinement and that the labor of creative resistance, as it occurs from below, is always at risk of being reabsorbed by power's new disordering ruses, its deployment of the immeasurable on behalf of exploitation. This chapter investigates the relation between this multivalent "labor of the head and heart" and film labor by attending to the rhythms through which they oppose "the elimination of the workday's 'pores' (that is, of 'dead' production time)" and, with it, the power to capture life at the level of the very labor of desire that could release it.[19]

Farocki's *Counter-Music* not only exposes but also subverts our enmeshed rhythms. My proposal for a counter-genealogy of film labor will thus pivot around it, while articulating itself in three partially overlying movements. First, I will show that Farocki meddles with our social factory by producing a rhythm that obstructs its seamless appropriation of the "workday's pores." The use of the split screen in a *soft montage* proves crucial in this respect, as it configures a rhythm that disturbs both the measure of industrial labor time and the "outside measure" harnessed by post-Fordism. I suggest that, by drawing on the notion of rhuthmos, we think of this rhythm as an arrangement that, in its very contingency and precariousness, does not fill time's pores but, rather, makes them visible as indeterminate openings. Second, I will advocate that, despite Farocki's direct quotations of Vertov, we trace the emergence of this other rhythmic impulse back to Italian Neorealism rather than the Russian avant-garde, to the sphere of domestic rather than industrial labor. In its adoption of soft montage, Farocki's investigation of labor connects most subtly not to Vertov's textile workers but to the young housemaid in De Sica's *Umberto D*. Finally, by way of a detour that touches on Jeanne Dielman's domestic routine, I will return to the film that constitutes Farocki's explicit reference point, Jean-Luc Godard's *Numéro deux* (*Number Two*, 1975). An essay on the complexities of cinematic *and* domestic production, *Numéro deux* occupies a critical place in our brief counter-genealogy. If industrial weaving stands as the metaphor for modern filmmaking (which is what Michelson claims apropos of Vertov), Godard does not simply offer us another metaphor, namely, film labor *as* housework.[20] Instead, he uses lateral variations, indeed typical of a certain kind of labor, in order to break with the very regime of hypermetaphoricity that had marked earlier theorizations. He proceeds by contiguity, disturbing theory's operation of substitution and its historically male coding with the more mundane operation of combination: metonymy instead of metaphor. If we were to remain in the world of textiles, then I would borrow from the title of a book by Luisa Muraro, *Maglia o uncinetto (To Knit or to Crochet)*, and suggest that both Godard and Farocki prefer to knit: to activate the gendered rivalry between metonymy and metaphor on behalf of the former.[21] However, they do so in a peculiar manner: by pushing metonymy beyond metonymy—that is, by spacing out its associative links, they perform a kind of knitting that primarily knits holes, spacing beyond measure.

Soft Montage

In what Farocki calls "soft montage," the use of a split or double screen enables two images to appear side by side, more or less simultaneously, and be edited also in relation to each other, rather than only in relation to the preceding and following ones. Farocki experimented with soft montage from the late nineties until his death in 2014, usually producing the same piece as both a two-monitor or split-screen installation and a single-channel film (in the latter case, the two images end up lightly overlapping in the center of the frame). Among the most celebrated examples of this practice, *Counter-Music* has received considerable attention, and yet the notion of soft montage itself has eluded sustained analysis, generating instead internally contradictory accounts.[22] As this doubling of the image complicates the way in which we think of rhythmic configurations, let me outline what I consider to be the main points of contention before advancing my own interpretation. Farocki himself first gestures toward a definition of soft montage in *Speaking about Godard,* coauthored with Kaja Silverman and organized as a dialogue between an image-maker and an image-theorist:

> When Godard shows two monitors, he makes one comment upon the other in a soft montage. I say "soft montage" since what is at issue is a general relatedness, rather than a strict opposition or equation. *Number Two* does not predetermine how the two images are to be connected; we must build up the associations ourselves in an ongoing way as the film unfolds.

According to Farocki, by letting one image comment on the other, Godard rejects the constraints of an "either-or" logic and comes to operate under the sign of the conjunction "and"—"'this' and 'that,'" specifies Silverman upon highlighting how video allows for the very simultaneity that film denies.[23] But are Farocki and Silverman speaking about Deleuze as well? They will quote him later, in a note to the chapter on *Passion* (1982), but it is hard not to invoke him here as he defines Godard's method as "the method of BETWEEN, 'between two images' ... the method of AND, 'this and then that.'"[24] In any case, the reference remains nebulous, especially because Farocki and Silverman seem to conceive of this method in terms of association. On the other hand, Deleuze explicitly states that the conjunction "AND" performs "not an operation of association but of differentiation ... or of disappearance," engendering something novel and irreducible to the combination of the preexisting images.[25] The tendency to regard this "AND" as conjunctive rather than disjunctive (a tendency which frequently returns in the literature on Godard and Farocki) obscures one of Deleuze's most

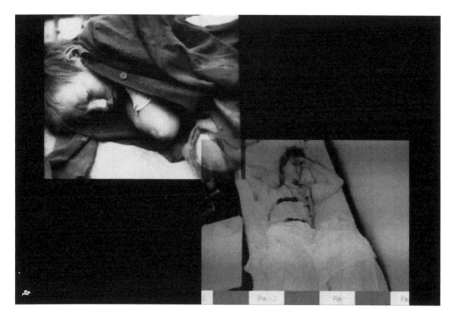

FIGURE 4. *Counter-Music* (Harun Farocki, 2004): the split screen of soft montage, or "more trial, less assertion."

vital intuitions.[26] In an interview on Godard's television series *Six fois deux* (*Six Times Two*, 1976), Deleuze was already emphasizing that what counts is not the number of images (two, three ...) but the conjunction: the force of the conjunction "AND" is that of the "border," of the "line of flight," along which "things come to pass, becomings evolve, revolutions take shape."[27] Later, in *Cinema 2*, he underscores that such an assemblage does not form a "chain of images." On the contrary, the interval marked by AND is precisely what enables cinema to break out of the chain, to flee, to find a line of flight: "it is not a matter of following a chain of images, even across voids, but of getting out of the chain or the association."[28] I believe that this tendency to privilege association over differentiation also accounts for the fact that, in some readings of *Counter-Music*, an almost direct line is drawn between Farocki and Vertov, as if the interval of soft montage were more or less a reprise of the Vertovian interval.[29] It is not. The latter amounts to a rational cut and "a correlation of two images which are distant," while soft montage develops out of Godard's method, which aims at producing an irrational or incommensurable cut, an "interstice" that is primary with respect to the images it brings together.[30]

In a later essay, "Cross Influence / Soft Montage," Farocki remains vague but, while insisting on the interplay of simultaneity and succession brought about by soft montage, points us in a direction that displaces and expands Deleuze's treatment of the interstice. He says:

> There is succession as well as simultaneity in a double projection, the relationship of an image to the one that follows as well as the one beside it; a relationship to the preceding as well as to the concurrent one. Imagine three double bonds jumping back and forth between the six carbon atoms of a benzene ring; I envisage the same ambiguity in relationship of an element in an image track to the one succeeding or accompanying it.[31]

What strikes me is that, by emphasizing intensity and ambiguity, Farocki brings into play both "force and meaning," as Christian Metz does when, in *The Imaginary Signifier,* he investigates the complexity of cinema's metaphorical and metonymical operations.[32] In a chapter on psychoanalysis and semiotics, Metz reaffirms that there exists an overlap (always imperfect, incomplete) between energetic relations and figures or trajectories of thought. Yet Metz is not ready to simply follow Jacques Lacan's theorization of metaphor and metonymy, or even Roman Jakobson's seminal essay on the topic: a good part of *The Imaginary Signifier* is devoted to clarifying what he considers the incorrect alignment between paradigm, metaphor, similarity, and condensation on the one hand, and syntagm, metonymy, contiguity, and displacement on the other. If reviewing his intricate argument exceeds the scope of this chapter, I will nonetheless mention that, for Metz, editing in itself is neither metonymical nor metaphorical: it is syntagmatic; and here we already see the way in which soft montage complicates the process, as it combines in the same shot images that would normally have followed one another. But the fact that they would have "substituted" one another on the horizontal axis (syntagm) does not entail that they were linked by similarity on the vertical axis (paradigm); this is simply a discursive operation, though one that has repercussions as to both ambiguity and intensity. Conversely, the fact that two images appear side by side does not preclude them from being linked by similarity rather than contiguity, although (again) this alignment complicates their relation.[33]

Deleuze turns to the workings of metaphor and metonymy while assessing the cinema of the movement-image, speaking of associative relations apropos of Sergei Eisenstein (metaphor) and D. W. Griffith (metonymy). However, he leaves them behind in his account of Godard's method, describing instead the un-linking of the figurative association, the re-linking of the (now) literal images, and the "new system of rhythm" (serial, atonal) that results from this operation, a system in which there is no sharp distinction between shot and montage.[34] But is this turning away from metaphor and metonymy the only way to test the limits of association and theorize cinema's renewed capacity for thought? In my inquiry, I want to remain close to these two modes of symbolic production (to work with what is at hand) as I take them to perform operations of thought that, at their most creative, transform the opposition between literal and figurative, real and imaginary, objective and subjective, et cetera; that is, I will remain in a domain where force and meaning work on each other, while also pursuing Deleuze's intuition on the disjunctive nature of the interval. If we take Jakobson and Metz seriously, then the images out of which the interval emerges relate to each other either metaphorically, metonymically, or in a mixed manner: what I will suggest is that the interstice produced by metonymy is different from the one produced by metaphor or, rather, that is it through a certain use of the metonymical that some of the more forceful intervals come into being. By forceful, I mean disruptive of the received associative paths and creative of a potential for new, unpredictable ones (rather than of explicit new ones). Soft montage then becomes the name for an experiment in audiovisual thinking that cannot be equated with any preset formal technique. Indeed, in "Cross Influence / Soft Montage," Farocki adds, "It seemed to me that although it is possible to do with one image everything one can do with two, it would still be easier to create a soft montage with two tracks. More trial, less assertion." I take this to suggest that soft montage does not require two tracks and that the nonrelational relatedness it engenders is in any case provisional, under construction (though more visibly so in the presence of a double track).[35]

Ultimately, for Metz, "the play of metonymy helps metaphors to emerge," but not vice versa. Against this bias on behalf of the metaphorical, I am interested in exploring what metonymy does—not in service but in excess of metaphor, what it does before or after it is taken up by metaphor.[36] In "To Knit or to Crochet," written in the aftermath of the

1970s feminist movement, Muraro invites us to tackle the effects of the "competition" ("in the sense of both collaboration and rivalry") between metaphor and metonymy as modes of symbolic production, rather than accept narratives of pacific collaboration.[37] In fact, the latter only disguises a process of domestication that has resulted in the long-held primacy of metaphor; and if Jakobson seems to grant both modes equal status, Lacan and the theoreticians of the "degree zero" do not, contributing to a regime of hypermetaphoricity that can think difference only by "passing through identity or equivalence."[38] The historical division of labor between these two operations can be outlined as follows: on the one hand, metaphor substitutes one term for another on the basis of similarity, inventing connections between disparate domains while transcending the specificities of experience; on the other hand, metonymy proceeds by contiguity, moving between terms that exist in a relation of material proximity and remaining within lived experience. "Thanks to metaphor," Muraro writes, "experience is reshaped as an ideal representation, while metonymy articulates experience into its parts."[39] Speaking a language requires both axes and modes of relation, although different personal or cultural styles might prioritize one over the other, as Jakobson suggests when he aligns metaphor with Romanticism and Symbolism, Surrealist painting, and the cinema of Eisenstein and Chaplin; and metonymy with Realist literature, Cubism, and the cinema of Griffith. However, a regime of uncontested hypermetaphoricity will keep us from "accept[ing] the new and the different as they present themselves."[40]

It is precisely metonymy's resistance to equivalence and identity that first made me wonder to what extent its operations can be productively mobilized on behalf of a rhythm that exceeds measure. It is my wager that, in *Counter-Music* as in *Numéro deux*, montage takes up the challenge of metonymy, attending to the relationship between images that are "nearby," contiguous in space and/or time. This is certainly not to say that in these films there are no metaphorical operations, and yet the bolder gestures are the more discreet ones, where the distance between images is somehow minimal but their divergence emerges as immeasurable. It is as if there were an inventiveness in proximity or a proximity to be *reinvented*: not the correlation of distant images but the distance, the divergence of adjacent ones, in a reworking of the relation between language and things that eludes equivalence or identity—an internal and dynamic creativity, a rearticulation of experience that, in our sociosymbolic order, doesn't come without strife.

ANOTHER WAKING UP

While *Counter-Music* opens with images of sleepers in Lille and in Vertov's composite city, I maintain that Farocki's soft montage does not lead us straight back to Vertov. What happened then between Vertov and Farocki? Vertov and Godard? The answer I propose is, "another waking up." Among the most celebrated sequences in the history of cinema, the awakening of the maid in *Umberto D.* is born "out of work," unfolding as a slow, trancelike reentry into the routine of domestic labor. A young woman tasked with all sorts of house chores, Maria sleeps on a cot in the hallway. She wakes up at dawn and, still drowsy, drags herself along the empty corridor and enters the kitchen. What follows is nothing less than a veritable choreography of domestic labor; the poetic documentation of a series of routine gestures, which the young woman performs without solution of continuity, almost sliding from one task to the next in a most efficient use of space and resources. The camera pans several times to keep her in sight as she walks around the kitchen table and (almost) stops to light a match, turn on the gas stove, take the kettle out of the cabinet, open the water faucet, drown the ants crawling above the sink, clear the table, put the kettle on the stove, look down, touch her pregnant belly, shed tears, sit on a chair to grind the coffee, and extend her leg to close the door. The sequence lasts over four minutes but contains only two reverse shots (glimpses of cats on the courtyard roofs) and few editing cuts. The latter mainly contributes to extending the camera's circular movements, at least until the end of the sequence, when Maria stretches her leg to close the door with the tip of her toe. During these last few moments, what we see is the emergence of a new gesture, a formal arrangement that is both of the woman's body and of the camera-editing system.

In "Images for Housework," Casarino attends to this sequence while rereading Deleuze's work on cinema in light not only of Spinoza but also of Italian feminism. Through a close analysis of specific sequences, he shows that, in both Visconti's *Ossessione* and De Sica's *Umberto D.*, the emergence

FIGURE 5. *Umberto D.* (Vittorio De Sica, 1952): Maria's variation on her daily choreography of housework.

FIGURE 6. *Umberto D.* (Vittorio De Sica, 1952): as Maria is balancing, an editing cut that is not needed.

Labor 53

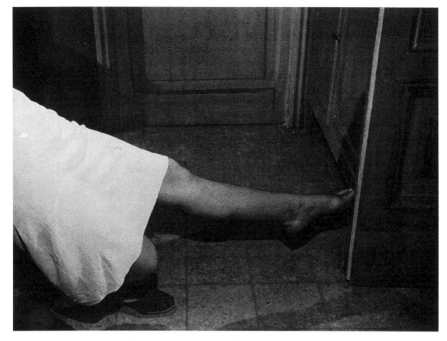

FIGURE 7. *Umberto D.* (Vittorio De Sica, 1952): Maria's acrobatic gesture, or "can she do it?"

of the time-image proves to be inseparable from the portrayal of domestic labor. "Housework," Casarino writes, "is the envelope, the before-during-after, of the time-image."[41] Neorealism finds in domestic labor not only a rich subject matter but also, and most important, the substance of an upsurge of time that reaches beyond movement. It is the maid scene that Deleuze mentions as the first example of a "pure optical situation" and that, before him, André Bazin describes in detail while discussing De Sica's art of duration:

> The camera confines itself to watching her doing her little chores: moving around the kitchen still half asleep, drowning the ants that have invaded the sink, grinding the coffee. . . . De Sica and Zavattini attempt to divide the event up into still smaller events and these into events smaller still, to the extreme limits of our capacity to perceive them in time. Thus, the unit event in a classical film would be "the maid's getting out of bed"; two or three brief shots would suffice to show this. De Sica replaces this narrative unit ["the maid's getting out of bed"] with a series of "smaller"

events: she wakes up; she crosses the hall; she drowns the ants; and so on. But let us examine just one of these. We see how the grinding of the coffee is divided in turn into a series of independent moments; for example, when she shuts the door with the tip of her outstretched foot. As it goes in on her the camera follows the movement of her leg so that the image finally concentrates on her toes feeling the surface of the door.[42]

Unlike Deleuze, Casarino follows Bazin in registering the fact that the scene ends with this almost acrobatic gesture, and not with the purely optical encounter between the maid's eyes and her pregnant belly—that is, the latter is fully enmeshed in the temporal fabric of housework.

What is crucial is that the sequence does not simply expose the quasi-mechanical dynamics of housework—in fact, it dares them. First of all, by virtue of a gesture that is not needed, touching the door with the tip of the toe, which Casarino considers an expression of potentiality, or what Giorgio Agamben calls "means without ends": a pure gesture in which "nothing is being produced or acted, but rather something is being endured and supported."[43] In the midst of her exhaustion, the young maid performs a gesture that, "as such," at once expresses her endurance and the potential for the world she lives in to be different from what it is. But then, I will argue, the sequence defies this order also by modulating the duration of the gesture in an impermanent, unsteady manner—by generating a rhythm that is both tentative and fluid, like a cautious leap, and marked by what, from the viewpoint of both housework and film editing, is sheer gratuitousness. In this respect, my interpretation departs from Casarino's reliance on Agamben and the latter's positing of gesture as interruption. I reclaim here the image as rhuthmos in light of the critique that I develop in the first chapter: rhuthmos upsets the fictitious equation of flow and continuity and, at the same time, does away with the thought of interruption as a stoppage of time, which ultimately remains a privilege of the (male) subject.

It is noteworthy that, in the passage on the maid, Bazin does not identify duration with the joint adoption of long take and depth of field. Instead, he points out that duration becomes manifest through a "division" of the conventional narrative unit (getting out of bed) into "smaller events" and of one among them (grinding the coffee) into "independent moments"—that is, through both camera movement and editing. If Bazin's lexical choices seem to indicate an understanding of discontinuity as composed of fractions and thus measurable, I will remark that these choices pertain to the film's narrative development rather than duration itself—dramatic time rather than "'life time.'"[44] When he speaks of actual duration, Bazin does so in terms of perception: what De Sica and screenwriter Cesare Zavattini test by dividing and thus also multiplying minimal events is "our capacity to perceive them in time." In other words, despite the adoption of quantitative terms, what Bazin describes is not a calculated, orderly partitioning of the event; it is not a "stretching" of duration. Rather, it is something like an internal proliferation, an efflorescence of time, less organic than chemical, the effect of the film's distinctive journey into time. Duration does not become "longer": it becomes immeasurable. Casarino, too, responds to this excess, which for him coincides with the eruption of the synchronic out of the diachronic: "To endure," he writes, "is not only to have a certain measurable, quantifiable duration but also to remain open to something immeasurable and unquantifiable in duration itself . . . *Can she do it?*"[45] Neither Bartleby's "I prefer not to" nor Akhmatova's "I can," this expression of potentiality—a question rather than an assertion—maintains language and perception in the openness of the future: it is not a matter of "*not* bring[ing] . . . knowledge into actuality" (as Agamben would say) but, rather, of not knowing in advance.[46]

What I specifically maintain is that, at the end of the sequence, duration emerges as immeasurable through the articulation of an erratic rhythmic cluster, the sketching of a configuration that neither reaches a climax nor coalesces into an organic whole. The appearing of this differentiated, rather than uniform, duration constitutes, in itself, an evasion of confinement and control, a break in the capturing of life. "Before anything else," writes Barthes in *How to Live Together*, "the first thing that power imposes is a rhythm (to everything: a rhythm of life, of time, of thought, of speech)."[47] The case of the mother dragging her child by the hand, to make him walk at her own pace (which Barthes reports as an occurrence he has observed on a precise date) points to the pervasiveness of this "domestication" of rhythm and the institutional reasons it serves beyond the sphere of production proper. On the other hand, rhuthmos as a fleeting, irregular form constitutes "the exact opposite of an inflexible, implacably regular cadence."[48] Here the ostensible translation of all rhythm into cadence functions to underscore rhuthmos's resistance to any kind of external ordering—a difference not of quantity but of quality. One could say that we find the child's delayed response in *Umberto D.*: set against the relentless routine of housework, the maid's gesture rediscovers this other rhythm, subtle and eccentric, emerging as one intermittent configuration rather than the sum of autonomous moments. Indeed, it is the moment that you can no longer see that is slipping away as a measuring unit. What you see is the configuration: rhythm beyond measure.

Falling, Fleeing

There is no gesture independent of the manner in which it is performed, which also means expressed by the camera and the editing. Four shots, caught between simultaneity and succession, articulate for us this gesture of defiance: while grinding the coffee, the young woman begins to stretch her leg, the camera panning to follow it; an edit reframes her torso as she slides toward the edge of the chair, elongating her whole body; then a slightly tighter shot of her leg as the tip of her toe reaches for and pushes the door; finally, a return to her upper body, as she steadies herself back into the chair, still grinding and crying, till the doorbell rings. It is pure potential that comes forth in this configuration of the gesture—in the gesture as a fluid and yet precarious, even hazardous configuration. But this idiosyncratic form does not belong to the figurative as opposed to the literal; it traverses and inhabits both domains. The maid is grinding the coffee and stretching her leg, doing what she is not expected to do, what is far from efficient—almost slipping but not quite. For us, it is not a matter of bridging the cut from one image to the other but rather, if you will, of remaining unsteadily suspended there, in the small gaps or slivers drawn by the edit. By reconfiguring this apparently homogeneous field, a field of labor and desire in which everything seems to have been woven in advance, the gesture of the maid—and of the camera-editing—sets the scene off-balance.

What is remarkable is that this setting-off-balance occurs without a leap into an overtly different field, like in the opening sequence of Chaplin's *Modern Times* (1936), where the shot of a flock of sheep is followed by the shot of a crowd of workers on their way to the factory. The maid scene almost falls off-balance not by virtue of a metaphorical operation but, rather, through the refiguring of what is near by means of what is also near, the everyday experience of the body—an exploration of proximity by means of proximity. In other words, by virtue of metonymy. In "To Knit or to Crochet," Muraro writes of the "division of labor" that, in our sociosymbolic order, has long relegated metonymy to an ancillary position. Against the demands of hypermetaphoricity, Muraro wants to reclaim metonymic language, which operates "via contact and contagion," as a mode of symbolic elaboration in its own right, one in which "the figurative meaning does not replace the literal one, since they are mutually supportive, nor do words tend to make things superfluous—one would in fact lose the meaning-effect if one lost sight of things."[49] I will soon return to this formidable text in some detail, but let me anticipate that what I have in mind is not quite the same. There is to metonymy a power of invention, of creative redefinition of borders, that occurs most forcefully when displacement by contiguity falls short of itself or—amounting to the same effect—reaches too far and, instead of an associative link, it produces a distance that cannot be measured or bridged. How far from the door are the leg and the foot? How far in space and time? What we see: a movement forward that folds on itself, a slow thrust, at once tentative and bold, less an arrow than an arch, or a bow . . . *can she do it?* True potential is released when the goal is not guaranteed, when failure might arise instead of success. There is risk, and here the young maid is no less courageous than Vertov's cameraman. She might fall—into oblivion, social death, or simply onto the floor, which can also hurt.

The sleepers in *Counter-Music* barely move and yet they, too, are at risk. Not of falling into the sewage system, the polluted nightmare of civil society, as the transition from the sleep lab to the city's underground corridors mischievously suggests (after all, Carol Reed's *The Third Man* [1949], too, is a city film). They are at risk of falling out of the unpredictable cracks of sleep, of dreaming according to preformed patterns, of dreaming as video gaming. What is under threat is that threshold between sleep and wakefulness that, as Jonathan Crary reminds us, constitutes not only a social affair but also the last barrier toward our ongoing loss of sociality. While writing about André Breton's description of Paris at daybreak in *Communicating Vessels*, Crary invites us to see the liminal zone between darkness and light as the site of "a collaboration yet to come between work and dreams, one that will animate 'the sweeping away of the capitalist world.'" Like the interval before sleep, the "suspended time" after sleep can play a transformative role with respect to our perceptual habits, enabling us to recover "a sensitivity or responsiveness to both internal and external sensations within a non-metric duration." The loosening of spatiotemporal coordinates that marks sleep and its border zones does not coincide with a withdrawal from history; on the contrary, as Percy Shelley and Gustave Courbet had intuited, it opens up the possibility of "another form of historical time," one in which "glimpses of an unlived life, of a postponed life, can edge faintly into awareness."[50] That several neorealist characters inhabit the world in a trancelike state, as Deleuze suggests when he calls *Ossessione*'s heroine "a visionary, a sleepwalker," points not to a retreat from our shared temporality but to a redefinition of it.[51] In the next chapter, I will return to this other temporality as it emerges in experiences of that oneiric wakefulness that cinema is most apt to express. Here I want to follow Agamben in emphasizing that "the original task of a genuine revolution . . . is never merely to 'change the world', but also—and above all—to 'change time'": without a novel conceptualization of time, even a revolutionary concept of history is bound to be reappropriated by ideology.[52]

In the opening sequence, Farocki's editing slides from shots of a nondescript street at dawn to images of sleepers in a sleep lab (in turn presented as prerecorded images, the "play" function visible at the bottom, and full-screen as direct images), sleep graphs, and clips from *Man with a Movie Camera* (see Figure 4). What is crucial is not only that it keeps sliding but also that it does so in a tentative manner. If the woman in Vertov's city knows little hesitation, her body rising as promptly as the city does, the sleepers in the lab barely get to open their eyes and offer us a hint of movement.[53] There is no thrust forward, no kinetic excitement here, as there is none in *Umberto D.*, which tells the story of a retired professor who lives in a state of abandonment; even the vague directionality of *Bicycle Thieves* has faded away. As a result, the attempt to correlate the graphs with the sleepers is less realized than displayed and, in the process, hindered: they align metonymically (both sets indexing the same phenomenon) while forming an arrangement (rhuthmos) that cannot be simply equated with a web of associations. Rather, they are held together in a "fissured" configuration, one that registers not only flashes of deep, vertical time (Vertov's woman is almost lying side by side with the lab sleepers) but also the disorderly proliferation of times inhabiting each present, finding in dispersion rather than unity the forms of a new aesthetic and political experimentation.

By intercutting shots of the woman, the cameraman (Vertov on his way to work), and the speeding trains with those of the lab, Farocki charges the latter with an energy they cannot release, an energy which then seeps through the crevices of the screen. It will take some time before we move past shots of the city's sewage system and the human body (the latter borrowed from Richard Fleischer's *Fantastic Voyage* [1966]) to reconnect to the hurtling trains. But even then this kinetic energy will find itself blocked, obstructed, as we are given shots of "image workers" in Lille's transportation control center, all barely moving in front of their computer screens. By now it is dawning on us that we, too, are part of this city of screen workers, relentlessly called on to look at images in a 24/7 economy. Yet, unlike them, here we are invited to see otherwise, to perform our labor differently. Several scholars have argued that *Counter-Music* at once exposes and alters the constraints imposed by this new regime of visuality, mobilizing "the image" against "the visual," to adopt Serge Daney's terminology.[54] For me, this means not only seeing in a noninstrumental manner but also in a manner that draws on the inventiveness of the metonymical—the capacity to produce gaps between parts that exist in a relation of proximity. I would add that this seeing beyond metonymy could also constitute a sort of "retraining" for the contemporary viewer. As we relentlessly shift from image to image following preordained associative paths, Farocki's montage is training us to see according to an interval or potential: rather than generating yet more associations, it shows us how to look for what lies in-between, what cuts across the ordinary or the unremarkable or the predictable. (Of course here I have in mind Benjamin's idea of cinema as training of the sensorium and suggesting that we need to reassess it in light of mutated historical conditions of production and reception.)[55] The force of soft montage is that of minimal distance.

THE IMPERFECT CHAIN

I am tempted to say that it is when she crosses her legs, while standing next to the stove and sipping the coffee she has just made: it is in this fleeting moment that Jeanne comes the closest to performing that gesture that is not needed, that gratuitous rearrangement of forms that had altered Maria's morning routine. In Chantal Akerman's *Jeanne Dielman, 23, Quai du Commerce, 1080 Bruxelles,* the story of a mother, housewife, and part-time prostitute, this gesture does not expand as much as it does in *Umberto D.,* and yet it throws things into a minor disarray, disturbing the balance of the character's body, which is now standing on one leg; the balance of her obsessive-compulsive way of inhabiting the world; and the balance of the film's composition and editing patterns, which mirror the character's desire for symmetry and regularity in a stance of "hyperbolic complicity," as Margulies has noted in her study on Akerman. Indeed, I agree with Margulies's claim that *Jeanne Dielman* is above all "a work about balance," and its force greatly derives from the "subversive equation of different orders of events": cooking, knitting, pouring coffee, murdering, et cetera.[56] However, my interpretation of this commitment to equivalence differs from that of Margulies, as does the attention I pay to what upsets it. Suspicious of the "detail" that stands out (Bazin's "grain of sand that gets into and seizes up a piece of machinery")[57] as the symptom of a wished-for totality, Margulies turns to the accumulation of minimalist art, borrowing the "et cetera" that strings together Jeanne's daily activities—her minor and major gestures, as if they belonged to the same order—from Rosalind Krauss's work on Sol LeWitt. Key to this reading is the attempt to offer an interpretation of autonomy that does not hinge on the subject's intentionality but that resides with a certain "animism" of objects (a brush, a button, a fork) as they seemingly start moving of their own accord on the second of this three-day chronicle. By contrast, I will reclaim the detail's power of intrusion not on behalf of but in opposition to the machinic order that has seized Jeanne's life.

Let me be clear: I am not suggesting that this first unwarranted gesture, this haphazard crossing of lines that violates the obsessive compulsive's obligation to geometry, brings about a resurgence of agency or hints to a fuller and yet still incomplete reality. What distinguishes this new bodily configuration is its singularity, the fact that it cannot be subsumed into the order that the film is exposing—exposing by repeating—and that Margulies aligns with the automatism of both minimalist art and obsession compulsion. That it remains uncertain whether this dislocation of the body is deliberate or not, a treat or a slip, only adds to its subtle and yet more radical subversive power. This other mode of subversion, which operates in the context of Akerman's "aesthetics of homogeneity" but also exceeds it, will resurface with a vengeance later the same day as Jeanne finds herself carried away in a whirlwind of uncoifed hair, faulty timing, and erratic movements. Margulies calls this sequence, in which Jeanne hurriedly carries around the apartment a pot of burned potatoes, "one of cinema's greatest choreographies of displaced anxiety," and it certainly is this, too.[58] But I would like to twist this reading and propose that we look at it as the emergence of a disorder, indeed of a disorderly configuration that breaks with the logic of equalization at work in the rest of the film. Here both film and character fret together for the first time, if only temporarily, in a manner that transforms the value of the conjunction "and," voiding its capacity for linking disparate events into "a seemingly endless and obsessional chain."[59]

We can surmise that something happens during the time Jeanne spends in her bedroom with a client (like the previous day, this scene remains conspicuously off-screen, an omission that is but the foil of the hypervisibility conferred to her domestic chores); in any case, we only see its aftereffects, and it is a tribute to Akerman's repurposing of the noir genre that we do not go looking for the alleged cause. Instead, we, too, are thrown into disarray as Jeanne fails to move with her habitual single-minded precision: most notably, she forgets to switch the lights on and off while going from room to room and helplessly fusses over the accidentally burned potatoes, not knowing how to dispose of them. This shift in pace and mood coincides with a palpable mutation in the formal balance of the film, that "litany of constricted forms" to which we had become accustomed: the camera is displaced to the other side of the kitchen and the editing becomes faster, even approximate in its attempt to follow the character's random meandering.[60] This disruption will not last long in terms of enunciation but will precipitate a domino effect in Jeanne's daily routine: the new potatoes do not cook in time for dinner, a fork she is drying drops to the floor, the brush skips out of her hand while she is cleaning her son's shoes, a button in her nightgown does not button, the coffee tastes bad, the scissors she inadvertently leaves on the bedroom's chest of drawers end up murdering the client with whom she has just had an orgasm, in a sex scene that is unexpectedly put on screen.

What Margulies finds transgressive in Akerman's "'blind' stringing together of cooking and killing" is the refusal to mobilize metaphor on behalf of abstraction and metonymy on behalf of totality.[61] (On the other hand, she detects the pitfalls of the latter in *Umberto D.* and of the former in Godard's *Two or Three Things I Know about Her.*) But this accumulation, as Krauss notes, this "babble" resembles "the loquaciousness of the speech of children or of the very old" and yet is not quite like them. On the contrary, this accretion of instances is "riddled with system, shot through with order."[62] Now, this "'system of compulsion'" certainly overwrites and thus bares as fictitious the requirements of pure thought, undoing the subject's primacy over the object. However, unless one believes in another kind of purity, that of the death drive, such a system does not function in radical defiance of measure and indeed needs measure in order to establish an equivalence between instances. What Jean-Joseph Goux calls the *general equivalent,* most notably money in the domain of commodities and the phallus in the domain of objects, imposes itself as the standard according to which things or people are valued and arranged hierarchically—or not. Jeanne's multiple position as a mother *and* a (widowed) wife *and* a prostitute conforms to rather than subverts the logic of abstract formalism that Irigaray was exposing at roughly the same time the film was made.[63] That Akerman pushes this formalism to an extreme—until cooking and killing can be reasonably put on the same plane—constitutes a remarkable subversion, one that makes this system slide on itself horizontally and loosens its joints. But it does not make them wobble.

What makes this system of compulsion quiver and almost fall out of joint are the details that cannot be strung together, as if something had gotten in between them that is of a disjunctive rather than conjunctive kind, not unlike what happens with soft montage. I have in mind the comedic dance of the burned potatoes and the barely perceptible vibrato of Jeanne's upper body during the seven minutes she spends sitting alone after the murder.[64] Here the pull of measure, rather than being exposed in its functioning or malfunctioning, falters in such a way that an excess is released—not the "purposeless purpose" of Krauss's minimalist art but something closer to the potential we have found in *Umberto D.*'s kitchen scene. In *Jeanne Dielman,* I maintain, it is a matter of light, of editing by means of light and darkness. Let's reconsider the much-remarked-on fact that Jeanne steadfastly switches the lights on and off whenever she leaves a room, and Akerman cuts to a new shot just a few seconds afterward.

For most of the film, these intervals in luminosity are put in place less to "preface" the cut than to stand "next to" and reinforce it, as if they were hinges guaranteeing that the right distance between gestures be preserved in space as well as time and at the level of both diegesis and enunciation. (What is imperative in the obsessive compulsive's world is not that things do not touch, as they have already at any rate, but that they remain spaced out in a predetermined, rigid manner.) But then something happens, and indeed *this* might be what happens: a mutation in the nature of the interval as the latter is taken over by contingency and stops providing the dead tissue, the steely net needed by the system of the obsessive compulsive. What happens is the irruption of randomness itself: the effect is also the cause.[65] At the end of the film, in a sequence that cannot simply be added to the preceding ones, we witness a similar transformation. The flickering neon light, which had been intruding in the living room every evening, no longer provides a scansion for Jeanne's movements and indeed loses power vis-à-vis Jeanne's irregular tremor. This scene endures as something other than a suspended ending. The latter still points toward an external, successive phase that would clarify or in any case expand the meaning of the scene we are witnessing. On the other hand, "these seven really very strong minutes after [the murder],"[66] as Akerman called them, constitute by themselves, in themselves, a singular configuration of being: rhuthmos as a form of life, if you will; sitting and trembling.

METONYMY BEYOND METONYMY

In this chapter I have argued that, while exploring spaces of urban inactivity and hi-tech labor, Farocki's soft montage bears the traces of a mode of editing that has been shaped through the portrayal of domestic labor. Godard's *Numéro deux* plays a key role in this counter-genealogy as it turns both editing and housework into the sites of a production that needs to be reimagined. The film comprises two prologues, a fictional part documenting the daily activities of a family in a housing estate, and an epilogue. All in all, I will suggest that *Numéro deux*'s investigation of labor *almost* unfolds as a sustained performance of metonymy—that it reworks the metonymical in order to generate incalculable intervals. In this respect, my reading differs from the one proposed by Farocki and Silverman, whose praise of the metaphorical runs the risk of stabilizing the film's subversive force. "But in spite of this repeated literal exposure of genitals, the seeing and showing of sexuality is heavily metaphoric," says Silverman apropos of the film's staging of the naked body in the domestic scenes. According to Silverman and Farocki, the vagina "becomes a metaphoric receptacle for memories," and the "metaphor of the mouth" is adopted to speak of the sexual organs, so that "to have sex is to kiss, or—better yet—to talk together."[67] But this is not quite the case. While the adoption of two video monitors characterizes most of *Numéro deux*, the scenes revolving around this "literal figuration" of the body play on a single monitor, surrounded by ample areas of black screen: Godard can eliminate the double monitor because his logic of the "two" finds expression in the characters' verbal exchange and the concurrent visibility of the body parts to which it points. Metonymy is key in both instances.

In the first scene, the camera focuses on the young daughter as she bathes, standing in the tub and washing her genitals, which occupy the center of the frame. The mother remains mostly off-screen, becoming partially visible only when she reaches out (into the frame) to help the daughter. Without interrupting what she is doing, the daughter asks, "Do all little girls have a hole?" to which the mother replies in the affirmative. Then she sits down, so that her head is now in the center, and calmly continues her inquiry: "Is that where memories comes out?" ("Of course," she is told) and, finally, "Where do memories go?" to which the mother's response is, "Into the landscape." What I find remarkable in the girl's reconfiguration of the body is that it proceeds by contiguity rather than similarity: the shift from the vagina as hole to the vagina as temporary holder for memories puts into play the head, which relates to the vagina metonymically rather than metaphorically. Like in the case of the expression "to think viscerally," the girl's suggestion that one remembers in and through the vagina entails a displacement within the body, between parts that, although hierarchically ordered in our culture, exist in a relation of spatial proximity. And there is a further displacement, enacted together with the mother: the hole though which memory flows is displaced onto the hole in the tub, so that memory now flows into the landscape in both a literal and figurative sense, becoming part of an expanded material network.

In the second scene, the camera portrays the parents as they lie naked on the bed and tell their children about the workings of sex. Pointing to her vulva, Sandrine asks, "See this? They're lips. My sex lips." Touching his penis, Pierre continues, "See here, it's a kind of mouth. And with this mouth, you kiss your lover's sex lips. Understand?" "And when we make love," Sandrine adds, "he puts his sex's mouth in the lips of my sex, as if we were kissing, as if we were talking. . . . It's called love. Love teaches us to talk." Here the sexual organs are explained by recourse to what is close by and also belonging to the body, the mouth and the lips. If anything, there is an entanglement or multiplication of body parts, not a substitution, and certainly not one that revolves around the mouth as unitary organ. Roughly at the same time the film was made, Luce Irigaray was writing that "her [the woman's] genitals are formed of two lips in continuous contact. Thus, within herself, she is already two—but not divisible into one(s)— that caress each other."[68] Godard's staging of sexual education mobilizes this same figure or, rather, mode of signification, producing what Muraro would call "a communication of a metonymic type, via contact and contagion," one in which literal and figurative meaning remain in a relation of productive interference.[69]

Why is it so important to specify that the body becomes the site of metonymic rather than metaphoric signification? After all, *Numéro deux* seems to offer us powerful metaphors: for instance, when the kids ask whether their dad and mum were "a factory or a landscape," and when Godard remarks that cinema is a factory. Muraro is helpful in this respect, too. She specifies that, even when the metonymical springs forth, the influence of the metaphorical cannot and indeed should not be excluded: what counts is using the metonymical differently, not getting rid of the metaphorical, as knitting takes two needles (Jakobson's two axes of language). What Muraro objects to is the "exploitation of metonymic resources" that has distinguished our regime of hypermetaphoricity, an order of semiotic production where "bodies, things, experience, nature, facts, are names of a blind spot and impracticable literalness."[70] While there is no spontaneous or immediate experience, there is a way of making sense of it (and thus, to some extent, also contributing to its unfolding) that wants to take some distance from the body and its intricacies. But this is not what Godard's didactic vignettes propose; on the contrary, here material being is both the subject and the object of the inquiry or, perhaps, something other, something that compromises the very distinction between the two.

"Pleasure is complicated," says the actor who plays the mother and wife. Metonymy, too, is not easy; it is a kind of labor and one that most often remains invisible in our sociosymbolic economy. Muraro explicitly writes of the "division of labor" that has traditionally characterized the relation between the metonymic and the metaphoric poles.[71] On the one hand, the task of substituting things with words, producing a system of representation in which the figurative replaces the literal, the universal subsumes the particular, and totality overcomes partiality: a system in which translation occurs on the basis of equivalence or identity. On the other hand, "the obscure task of gluing things to words," of making sense contextually and materially, thus allegedly discovering rather than inventing relations.[72] If this latter task proves to be indispensable for the workings of the former, all the more reason to diminish it and keep it hidden, make it disappear in the cracks of daily life, and insist that without the former there is no effective symbolization—that illness awaits just around the corner. Freud's hysteric is, after all, affected by the incapacity to read metaphorically, and Lacan's subject would be condemned to either senseless drifting or paralyzing immobility if it did not process symbolic castration. But for Muraro, who rereads Jakobson in light of Irigaray, "metonymic language is a mode of symbolic elaboration" in its own right, one that is capable of making sense of the concrete *and* the abstract: of mobilizing the concrete to point to the insufficiencies of the abstract.[73] Indeed, "the metonymic directrix, which is foreign to [the metaphoric directrix's] ascending motion, hinders it, cuts across it, prevents it from arriving at its logical conclusion—which would be that of gathering itself in a name, like the All, Being, God, and then silence."[74] When it resists normalization, the metonymic releases its own power of invention. It happens, for instance, in Virginia Woolf's lecture "Women and the Novel," which Muraro calls her first "discourse on method." On this occasion, "what the world showed of itself is one of its constitutive characteristics, namely, its possibility to be other. Which is to say: a sum of differences that are continuously becoming."[75]

It is this very potential that *Numéro deux* attempts to release. That it does so by showing scenes of domestic life and its everyday chores is more than mere chance. After all, the material and immaterial tasks that fall under the rubric of "housework" have been long positioned outside the sphere of production proper and those responsible for it relegated to invisibility. But what the film does with this most timely choice of topic (Akerman's *Jeanne*

Dielman was released the same year) is equally crucial: it proceeds along the metonymic directrix—that is, it repeats at the level of form the mode of labor that it sets out to explore. Take, for instance, the long sequence portraying the grandmother's activities: peeling vegetables, making the bed, washing the floor, ironing, and cleaning herself. All activities except the last one (which occurs in front of the bathroom mirror) appear on two video monitors in an arrangement that plays with succession and simultaneity: on the left, a larger screen shows an activity for the first time; on the right, a smaller screen displays the same activity after it has disappeared from the main screen, generating a sort of echo.[76] It is as if, faced with the task of defining housework, Godard could not give us a synonym or a metaphor or even a simple metonymy. The husband will later declare that "home is a factory" for his wife and, in the film's double prologue, we hear Godard speak of cinema itself as a factory. But, in this crucial sequence, it is as if Godard eschewed substitution; as if, like the "female patient" of whom Jakobson writes, he were incapable of metaphorization. Instead, he performs a series of metonymies—metonymies for housework.

As I am proposing that we rethink what Deleuze calls Godard's "stammering" in terms of aphasia, it is worth returning directly to Jakobson's treatment of the topic.[77] In describing the "similarity disorder" as the type of aphasia that impairs the operations of selection and substitution (along the paradigmatic axis), Jakobson specifies that such a loss in the "capacity of naming" brings about a loss in metalanguage but, to varying degrees, spares context-bound words such as deictics (for instance, pronouns and pronominal adverbs). This disturbance touches on the very integrity of the code. Referring to Goldstein's tests, he writes:

> A female patient, when asked to list a few names of animals, disposed them in the same order in which she has seen them in the zoo; similarly, despite instructions to arrange certain objects according to color, size, and shape, she classified them on the basis of their spatial contiguity as home things, office materials, etc. and justified this grouping by reference to *a display window* "where it does not matter what things are" (they do not have to be similar).[78]

I find this picture most instructive precisely as a *picture,* that is, a semiotic assemblage that exceeds the verbal domain. Not only does it give us a mode of arrangement that is inseparable from specific experiences, but it also mobilizes semiotic diversity, the perceptual world persisting even when the so-called direct experience has ended. It mixes words and things; it is impure; it operates by abundance, excess (like Barthes's "third meaning"), producing a configuration of signs where a normal speaker would have used a single word or associated between two words by substituting on the basis of similarity. In this picture, the many cannot be subsumed under the one and, concurrently, their coming-together, their arrangement, cannot be divided into independent elements. This is also the case in Godard's metonymic portrayal of the grandmother. What we are given in place of discrete signs is a configuration, a mode of appearing in which color, size, and shape cannot shake off their contingency—their rhythm (rhuthmos), if you will. This new contingent sign cannot be substituted with a preexisting one, cannot be added to the code without interrupting or at least disturbing the way the latter works.

For Jakobson, all sign systems share language's fundamental axes or modes of arrangement (selection/substitution and combination) and, concomitantly, mobilize the metaphoric and metonymic processes to varying degrees in order to develop a discourse.[79] In the last part of the essay on aphasia, he gives examples of tendencies or styles based on the dominance of one pole or the other in verbal art, painting, and cinema. The latter seems to constitute a special case, since Jakobson recognizes that, since D. W. Griffith, cinema has shown a general preference for the metonymical (Charlie Chaplin and Sergei Eisenstein's montage would constitute an example in the other direction). And yet Godard's metonymies are not Griffith's, and here my reading of Muraro is inflected by Deleuze and his emphasis on the disjunctive nature of the irrational cut. It is my wager that Godard's metonymies do not quite "glue" things and signs; that, in *Numéro deux*, we find a use of metonymy that makes the chain of associations malfunction and even break where things that exist in proximity are usually bound together—sutured—and put to use on behalf of the same. The persistence of the black screen, its being a constitutive part of the frame, together with the insistence on repetition, concur to turn the metonymic juxtapositions into a fissured configuration. If an "escape from sameness to contiguity" already marks the similarity disorder in which speaking does not pass through identity or equivalence, here a more radical escape or fleeing occurs in the fissure separating one monitor from the other and one shot from the other.[80] The "and" of metonymy becomes rhuthmos: a configuration that bears the marks of contingency without complying with it, a potential springing forth from within contingency, its cuts and pleats. "Numéro trois"—her place—is this potential.

It is the female actor, Sandrine Battistella, who pronounces these lines in the film's epilogue: "Finally in my place. Number three." Indeed, in the course of the film, Sandrine's voice and image have gradually displaced Godard's as operators of material and symbolic production. In the first prologue, the director appears amid his editing machines, "in person" and through a live feed that doubles his image on an adjacent monitor. In the second prologue, Godard has disappeared and we see two video monitors, stacked vertically on top of each other, and hear Sandrine as she continues Godard's meditation on cinema by introducing a more explicit concern with the number two.[81] She speaks as the female actor of the film, wondering whether *Numéro deux* is a film about "sex or politics," only to immediately add, "Why is it always either-or? It can be both sometimes." She also questions the preference given to the "once" in storytelling, defending the cause of the "twice," the double or repetition. Finally, in the epilogue, Godard reappears in the editing studio, this time sitting almost motionless: a spectator of the family scenes replaying on the video monitors and a listener to Sandrine's recorded voice. After her character has come to know the vicissitudes of other women, the actress now reflects on what it means for women to speak for themselves, to tell their own stories directly, to invent their own grammar. This is the final phase in what Silverman calls Godard's process of authorial divestiture or self-erasure, which in my reading of the film occurs through the weaving of a disjointed metonymic texture.[82] It is by attending to the pole of metonymy, by thinking "viscerally," that Godard comes to find himself closer to the wife, the grandmother, and the daughter than to the husband, the grandfather, and the son—closer to Yelizaveta Svilova than to Vertov. This might only be a temporary realignment but, as it occurs in the mode of repetition, it cannot stop having happened. The husband's metaphors, the grandfather's master narratives, the son's solitude have all been displaced through the workings of metonymy beyond metonymy. "Two" has become "three," the place of reinvention: "this and that" without interlocking, without chains. In the process, a countergenealogy of filmmaking has emerged: editing *and* housework.

3. Memory

"MONTAGE IS A HEARTBEAT"

In a 1956 article titled "Montage, mon beau souci," Jean-Luc Godard invites us to conceive of montage and direction *(mise-en-scène)* as irreducibly intertwined. "Only at peril," he writes, "can one be separated from the other. One might as well try to separate the rhythm from the melody." And then, in the aphoristic fashion that will soon distinguish his critical interventions, he adds, "If direction is a look, montage is a heartbeat."[1] In the rest of the article, Godard presents us with several convincing, if still limited, examples of such an interlacing, but none of them, so to speak, gets to our heart. It is Alain Resnais who, more than twenty years later, will realize the simplest and most effective translation of Godard's insight on montage and rhythm. His *Mon oncle d'Amérique* (*My American Uncle,* 1980)—a film that cares for montage like few others—opens with a veritable tribute to the intermittencies of our being: a stylized red heart, a heart that pulsates against a black background, appearing and disappearing at regular intervals, setting a beat for the film to play with and subvert. The three characters' memories and desires will develop in response to this heartbeat, a pulsation that will lose its evenness as the film edits together excerpts from French cinema (classics featuring Danielle Darrieux, Jean Marais, and Jean Gabin) and its own original scenes. Indeed, one could say that the film will find its singular heartbeat by weaving together the characters' disparate attempts to find their own—to love according to their own rhythm, in a field of desire that has been shaped by memories in excess of any individual life span. I would like to take Godard's assertion, together with Resnais's animated image, as points of departure for what I will attempt do in this chapter: delineate the contours of a short history of montage. This history will focus on the role that montage can play in expanding perception and liberating a renewed capacity for memory, including the memory of forgotten futures, when it turns itself into an idiosyncratic modulation of the sensible.

I envision this history as fragmentary, discontinuous, and deliberately tactical—a history written in response to what Bernard Stiegler calls the "disorientation" or "becoming-ill" of contemporary culture.[2] Under the economic imperative of "saving" time, Stiegler argues, the current media system promotes only what neutralizes distance and flattens out time. Such a reduction of spatiotemporal difference has precipitated a loss of individuation at the level of both individual and collective consciousness, one that threatens our ability not only to remember the past but also to imagine a future that does not resemble the present. Indeed, it is the very temporality of consciousness that has become the object of systematic exploitation. Today's audiovisual technologies, states Stiegler in what marks a significant shift of emphasis from memory to rhythm, control "the conscious and unconscious rhythms of bodies and souls."[3] They impose a homogeneous patterning of time and reduce the alternation of *otium* and *negotium*—our essential "being-in-intermittence"—to an economy of uninterrupted labor.[4] The mass synchronization denounced in the third volume of *Technics and Time* acquires in Stiegler's later work a more menacing power, as it now pertains to the level of a general rhythmics. In *Technics and Time,* synchronization was still equated with the simultaneous exposure to media programming, as in the case of the old broadcasting system, an equation that did not account for the more personalized viewing habits introduced by digital television, on-demand viewing, and Internet streaming. Synchronizing ostensibly heterogeneous habits falls instead under what Gilles Deleuze and Félix Guattari have called the "axiomatic of capital," that is, capital's capacity to produce isomorphy across wide-ranging scenarios rather than homogeneity proper.[5] Drawing on André Leroi-Gourhan's work on aesthetics, Stiegler now distinguishes between three kinds of rhythm: biological or physiological, technical or technological, and cultural or figurative. It is the interplay between these rhythms that guarantees our specific individuation as subjects of consciousness: "'I am a singularity,'" writes Stiegler, "means that *I give myself my own time*," that "my consciousness . . . *is not synchronized with yours.*"[6] In other words, a certain modulation of perception is the precondition for attaining that process of individuation without which no singularity is possible. Hyperindustrial societies de-individuate consciousness and thus de-singularize our being by standardizing our aesthetic rhythms and synchronizing them to an unprecedented degree. In the age of hypervideo technologies, the individual becomes a "dividual."[7]

Far from jettisoning audiovisual media altogether, Stiegler celebrates cinema for its capacity to enrich the workings of perception and memory. His analysis already points to some of the films that a short history of montage will eventually include Federico Fellini's *Intervista* (*Interview*, 1987), Resnais's *Mon oncle d'Amérique*, and Michelangelo Antonioni's *L'Eclisse* (*The Eclipse*, 1962). However, his reasons for praising these films differ from mine, and this is where my proposal betrays its own theoretical investment. For Stiegler, cinema owes its extraordinary force as *pharmakon* (both poison and remedy) to the fact that montage reaffirms the operations of consciousness as a coalescing and self-aggregating flow. "Consciousness," he writes, "is thoroughly cinematographic," in the sense that it constitutively operates according to criteria of selection and combination that are proper to film editing.[8] At the cinema, the spectator's consciousness "is captured and 'channeled' by the flow of images," relinquishing its own time to the time of its temporal object (the film), partaking of a rhythm that is off sync with its own and yet ultimately unifying.[9] For Stiegler, perceptual surrender continues to occur under the auspices of a single flux. To be fair, such a flux resembles not a line but "a tissue or a weave," even a "whirling spiral," as the subject is always inhabited by unconscious memories and formed by a heritage or past that it has not directly lived. Still, this is a flux that aims at becoming-one—that is, "in-dividual."[10]

This is for me a crucial point. On the one hand, by stating that "perception is cinema," Stiegler posits a subject that is originally prosthetic, exterior to itself, and thus always traversed and potentially undone by all kinds of memory.[11] On the other hand, he immediately domesticates the scope and modalities of this process of transindividuation by turning it into the discrete relation between intending subject and intended object (to the point that the unconscious, too, is ultimately conceived on this model).[12] It is as subjects vis-à-vis objects that the *I* and the *we* find themselves mutually individuated and come to form a particular ethnic community. His brief reading of *Mon oncle d'Amérique* is symptomatic in this respect. While discussing the phantasmatic structure of perception, Stiegler highlights how Resnais's film revolves around the alignment between its three main characters and their film idols (Darrieux, Marais, and Gabin). Such an alignment at once exposes and realizes that interlacing of perception and memory, reality and fiction, lived and imagined experience that constitutes life's richness. Yet without attending to specific montage sequences, Stiegler misses the emergence of a more intricate and dispersed fabric, one in which plants and animals play as conspicuous a role as the French actors, and the film could be said to experiment with what Donna Haraway will call "tentacular thinking."[13] At the beginning, for instance, the recurring shots of algae, rocks, crabs, and turtles are part and parcel of the protagonists' prehistory, as the scientist's voice-over reminds us of a process of evolution that did not begin (or end) with us. Throughout the film, there emerges a heterogeneity that is due not to a multiplication of self-enclosed characters and storylines but to their dispersion, their turning into configurations of movements, colors, and sounds in excess of any strictly defined *I* or *we*. "*We* all know the songs being played here—'we,' that is, the audience *living in France*," comments Stiegler apropos of Resnais's *On connaît la chanson* (*Same Old Song*, 1997), a virtuoso film in which the characters break into lip-synced songs. "It is hard to imagine," he adds, "that someone watching this film who had never lived in France, and knew nothing, therefore, of its *popular culture*, would be able to see it."[14] I would add that it is hard not to read in these statements the claim that belonging to a community needs to be predicated on exclusivity and continuity, no matter how many voices are ignored or dubbed in the process of securing it.

In this chapter, my perplexity regarding Stiegler's aesthetic and political move on behalf of cultural cohesiveness takes on a specific formulation.[15] Is the conflation of editing and consciousness ultimately productive as we attempt to counter the ongoing reduction of our aesthetic rhythms and concurrent depletion of sensibility? What is left of that indetermination without which life becomes already lived in advance, once we have decided that perception and memory operate—and should continue to operate—at the level of intentional consciousness? In addressing these questions, I will turn to Walter Benjamin's work, which Stiegler mentions only in passing, as it, too, expresses deep concern with the impoverishment of experience promoted by new technical media and yet leaves room for modes of individuation that reach beyond the subject-object relationship. What I will attempt to recover in Benjamin's controversial notion of aura is not an "experience without a subject," the return to a state of confusion prior to the split between subject and object, but rather the experience of a differentiation that cannot be reduced to such a split.[16] More specifically, I will propose that we reconceive of the aura as the emergence of a certain *rhythm*—a modulation of the sensible that upsets fixed positions, autonomous contours, and measurable intervals. This constitutes a novel interpretation, which I will develop by tracing Benjamin's own rhythmic disposition and, at the same time, returning to the notion of *rhuthmos* as fluctuation to foreground the paradoxical relationship between permanence and impermanence, persistence and transience.[17] It is as an irregular rhythmic patterning or configuration of perception that the aura blurs the boundaries between subject and object, enabling other unexpected formations to emerge. Finally, I will show that cinematic montage proves key in eliciting the auratic experience to the extent that it, too, embraces rhythm as idiosyncratic arrangement. Editing according to the fugitivity of forms can help renovate not only the contents of our memory archive but also the process of differentiation, the rhythm through which our subjectivity comes into being—perhaps to rediscover subjectivity itself as rhythmic differentiation.

Godard's *Contempt* (*Le Mépris,* 1963) and David Lynch's *Mulholland Drive* (2001) stand out among the films that perform this complex function, which Miriam Hansen would describe as at once critical and redemptive.[18] Like Resnais's *Mon oncle d'Amérique,* both films revolve around the vicissitudes of cinema as an apparatus for the production and reception of images, thus bearing the promise of a memory *en abyme*: the memory of the memory that cinema has engendered in the first century of its existence. In addition, both films present us with montage sequences (the "projection room" and the "jitterbug dance") that bring about a return of the auratic as the emergence of rhythms capable of resisting the compression of our temporal and spatial horizons. In these sequences, rhythm becomes rhuthmos in a displacement of the beat, time's measuring unit, and the surfacing of a discrepancy between sound and image that cannot be woven back by or on behalf of the subject. In their affirmation of an elusive and yet persistent memory, these two films contribute to delineating a constellation, a nascent force field for a history of montage as the experience of that oneiric wakefulness, that openness to metamorphoses that one better tolerates in dreams. (This history, let me remark, should be written many times over, and by many different hands.)

THE AURA AS RHYTHM

The question of whether cinema can assert itself as an auratic medium while also playing a subversive political role has received widespread attention, most notably in Miriam Hansen's sustained study of the Benjaminian corpus.[19] In Benjamin's work, *Erfahrung*—experience in the expansive sense—acquires its multifaceted meaning in opposition to *Erlebnis*—instantaneous, isolated experience.[20] Yet it would be reductive to simply associate the latter with cinema and the liquidation of the aura, and the former with traditional aesthetic practices; or to automatically realign cinema and deep experience *(Erfahrung)*, as if technical media had not produced a reorganization of perception. Hansen maintains that antinomies drive Benjamin's thinking, signaling the contradictions at the core of modernity, but that his stance also remains productively ambiguous, irreducible to the clear-cut opposition of "liquidationist" and "culturally conservative."[21] Indeed, she repeatedly shows that Benjamin's thinking mobilizes a field of concepts (aura, mimesis, optical unconscious, among others) whose value is relational and mutable, dependent on the particular constellation animating each text. In this context, I am interested in tracing how Benjamin's conflictual reflection on cinema and experience finds its pivot in the joint questions of rhythm and montage, pointing to different conceptualizations of what montage *as* rhythm is and can do.

In the artwork essay, the advent of film at once highlights and brings to fruition a process that has marked the history of modernity, namely, the disintegration of the aura. As "a strange tissue of space and time: the unique apparition of a distance, however near it may be," the aura eludes any substantive definition and yet, precisely as such, delineates the sphere of intervention for a politics of art that has the masses as its subject.[22] In the age of technical reproducibility, perception—by filmmakers and film spectators alike—aims at "getting closer" to things, at eliminating the distance that separates the object not only from its viewers but also from itself.[23] Such a desire to bring the object closer, to assimilate or incorporate it into one's own space, coincides with the desire to "make it present," to bring it into one's own time. The passage continues: "To follow with the eye—while resting on a summer afternoon—a mountain range on the horizon or a branch that casts its shadows on the beholder is to breathe the aura of those mountains, of that branch."[24] The aura does not belong to the natural object or the artwork or the face in the daguerreotype; rather, as Hansen emphasizes, it "pertains to the *medium* of perception," becoming itself a medium of relationality, one that "envelops and physically connects—and thus blurs the boundaries between—subject and object, suggesting a sensory, embodied mode of perception."[25] The auratic experience exceeds the strictures of the optical, animating the viewer's entire corporeal being: the subject is not only seeing, she is also breathing. Let me develop this reading further. In the passage, seeing itself is not simply accompanied by breathing: "to follow with the eye ... is to breathe"—seeing *is* also breathing, that is, partaking of a certain rhythm and being taken by that rhythm, as in the practice of yoga, to which Benjamin devotes some attention. In the age of mechanical recording, I will suggest, what is lost together with the interplay of nearness and remoteness in the experience of contemplation is also a certain rhythm, a certain way of inhabiting the fabric of the sensible.[26] Indeed, this is not the first time that Benjamin connects contemplation and the rhythm of breathing. In the epistemo-critical prologue to *The Origin of German Tragic Drama,* Benjamin defines the encounter between critique and its object as an alternation of withdrawals and returns, a nearing that is also a taking leave. "This continual pausing for breath," he writes, "is the method most proper to the process of contemplation." For the young Benjamin, the task of "philosophizing beyond philosophy," which he pursued before turning his attention to technical media, entails the deployment of fragments and, together with it, the assumption of an "irregular rhythm."[27]

In the rest of the artwork essay, however, film seems to offer us "training" for a world that has no time for this kind of rhythm. On the contrary, it can help us adjust and respond to our mutated conditions of existence because it shares some of their aggressive, overwhelming paces. An apparatus that thrives on fragmentation and revisability, film can retrain the human sensorium and hopefully enable the masses to see themselves critically. Montage plays the pivotal role: changes in framing, speed, and point of view only acquire relevance in the context of the discontinuous continuity—the assemblage—that constitutes the edited film. "The work of art," states Benjamin, "is produced only by means of montage."[28] It is precisely the "shock character" of montage, its "percussive" rhythm, that prevents the spectators from engaging with the images on-screen in the mode of contemplation and absorption typical of the auratic, fostering instead a process of "reception in distraction," a response that builds on the tactile rather than optical components of perception. Closer to architecture than to painting, cinema can reveal the hidden fabric of our daily lives (what Benjamin calls the *optical unconscious*) and thus engender a new vision on behalf of the collective. Yet it is here that Benjamin's argument regarding the destruction of the aura as unique distance also encounters one of its limits—the unconscious, psychoanalysis tells us, can never be made fully present, brought into absolute proximity, rendered "equal" to consciousness. As Hansen observes, "The optical unconscious marks a spot that readmits dimensions of temporality and memory via, and into, the very technologies capable of eliminating them."[29]

On the other hand, in the Baudelaire essay, Benjamin criticizes modernity precisely as the epoch that enacts "the disintegration of the aura in the experience of shock."[30] He directly aligns technical media with shock and a radical loss of memory, at both the individual and collective level. "In a film," he writes, "perception in the form of shocks was established as a formal principle." And again, "that which determines the rhythm of production on a conveyor belt is the basis of the rhythm of reception in the film."[31] Montage gives us the pivot around which production and reception come to double each other, and such a pivot is of a strictly rhythmic kind. In its implacable cadence, film repeats in the sphere of reception what is already happening in the sphere of industrial production and amid the city crowds—a relentless assault on the human sensorium, an attack to which consciousness tries to respond by raising its "protective shield" and assigning to the excessive stimuli a precise place in time. But the repetition performed by cinematic montage is neither therapeutic nor revelatory with respect to the shocks of everyday life. In contrast, it adds to the impoverishment of experience in the emphatic sense *(Erfahrung)*, relegating the sense impressions we receive to "a certain hour in one's life [*Erlebnis*]," that is, to experience in the reductive sense of short-lived involvement.[32] If, in the artwork essay and other writings, a certain "poverty" of experience was welcome to the extent that it shattered bourgeois values, here the decline of authentic experience threatens our very capacity for memory, what Hansen defines as the capacity "to remember both past sufferings and forgotten futures."[33] Cinema and photography can enrich the archive of voluntary, discursive memory but prove useless for the purposes of involuntary memory and indeed contribute to its erosion.

What renders cinema and photography incompatible with remembrance is, together with their rehearsal of the shock effect, their inability to return our look. "The camera," Benjamin notes, "records our likeness without returning our gaze," thus reinforcing (rather than transforming) the separation between subject and object. In this essay, we encounter a novel definition of aura as the web of associations that gather around the object of perception when this object is endowed with the ability to look back at us. Benjamin writes:

> Experience of the aura thus rests on the transposition of a response common in human relationships to the relationship between the inanimate or natural object and man. The person we look at, or who feels he is being looked at, looks at us in return. To perceive the aura of an object we look at means to invest it with the ability to look at us in return. This experience corresponds to the data of the *mémoire involontaire*.[34]

This interpretation of the auratic as a visual experience of deep time (the time where involuntary memory is nested) cannot but reverberate with the artwork essay's definition of the aura as "the unique apparition of a distance." Hansen's interpretative gamble proves crucial precisely at this juncture. As a form of responsiveness that hinges on and mobilizes the associations of involuntary memory, the aura coincides with the appearance of a distance that is also *temporal*.[35] In the auratic experience, we rediscover the lost temporality of things, as if solicited by a capacity for vision that already lies hidden in them.[36] It is a form of surrender, a responsiveness through which our spatiotemporal hinges are momentarily undone and, together with them, our very sense of self. In fact, the look that is returned to us is not contemporary with the present of the perceptual exchange, but reaches us from the depth of a time in excess of chronology. Not only do we face a forgotten or alien self but also come to remember what we have not lived directly, perhaps even what has never happened. An experience in the sense of *Erfahrung*, this memory does not possess an orderly or cumulative structure—instead, like Penelope's yarn and Proust's involuntary memory, it is punctuated by, interwoven with, forgetting.[37]

The auratic, as emergence of a unique spatiotemporal distance, entails a mutation, however transient, in the articulation of the perceptual field, a redefinition that coincides with a turning back, a return of the look toward what will have become other. Such a redefinition does not occur all at once—while the return of the look exceeds linear temporality (it is not a matter of succession or alternation), nonetheless it still unfolds in time. Would it then be implausible to suggest that the auratic, as it appears in Benjamin's description of lyric poetry and early photography, inaugurates the emergence of a certain *rhythm*? In order to distinguish auratic rhythm from the rhythms that occlude it, I return to the pre-Socratic notion of rhythm as rhuthmos: "configuration," "disposition," or "form." In this early and widespread sense of the term, rhythm is a form that is inseparable from the time of its appearance, a form that does not coalesce, a fluctuating form. Before becoming order in movement, rhythm is a "particular manner of flowing," an arrangement whose ephemeral irregularity is not evaluated on the basis of an external measure.

DISPLACING THE BEAT

In "The Echo of the Subject," Philippe Lacoue-Labarthe emphasizes that it is in this original sense—as a crucial trait in "the general differentiation of what is"—that rhythm can sustain the problematic of the de-constitution of the subject, the emergence of a subject that "comes to itself only in losing itself."[38] In the first chapter, I began to discuss how Lacoue-Labarthe turns to rhuthmos in the endeavor to go back "from Narcissus to Echo," from reflection to resonance, while addressing Reik's writings. In the modality of rhuthmos, or, rather, in rhuthmos as a modality of the form, he discovers "something pre-specular," which enables him to posit repetition, "the repeated difference-from-itself of the Same," as constitutive of the subject and its desistance.[39] Always situated between the visible and the audible (Echo is never far from Narcissus), vision itself leaks out of the framework of stability and identity through which it had been defined. In this newly found radical elusiveness, Lacoue-Labarthe reaches beyond Reik, treating the question of rhythm as separate from that of music and thus opening up a field of latent and unpredictable mutations. In Reik's work, rhythm is still essentially musical, bound to what Émile Benveniste has called "the law of numbers."[40] For instance, Reik speaks of "personal rhythm" and agreement between rhythms ("the ideal of love as 'two hearts and one beat'"), to the point of envisioning a "general rhythmics," a modulation of the affective, pulsional register that extends to society as a whole.[41] Yet in moving from the musical to the social, he relies on the notion of tact and its fundamental relation to time and measure: "*Takt* means time as counted and consolidated in units."[42] He remains within a domain that has already undergone a certain partitioning, namely, the division of the visible and the audible. On the other hand, by returning to rhuthmos, Lacoue-Labarthe repositions the question of subjectivity at the unmeasurable cusp of sensorial differentiation, in a caesura that is of both thought and experience.

It is here that we might also find some alternative to the "percussive" model of subject formation proposed by John Mowitt in his study of rock and roll as a "rhythmic 'event.'"[43] For Mowitt, rhythm enables us to "make sense of otherwise senseless beating," to respond to and resist the often violent, brutal solicitations that occur through skin contact.[44] Crucial to his argument are the historical conditions under which this rhythmic sense-making has developed—namely, the transatlantic slave trade, the African American migration from the rural South to the industrial North, and the systemic violence perpetrated against the Black community in the growing urban centers. Nonetheless, sense-making is defined as "rhythmic" only insofar as it is "percussive"—that is, accomplished through the beat (and backbeat) of drumming and thus regulated by the convergence of "time and measure."[45] Drumming (beating, striking) marks the emergence of the subject in a field where the musical beat, the shocks of modernity, and the psychoanalytic fantasy of beating find themselves interlocked in repeated performances of historical violence *and* resistance. In the percussive field of the city, Benjamin's lyric poet figures as the hero who responds to shock by "parrying the blows" and "letting go," becoming a conduit for the emergence of auratic memories; in this intermingling of active and passive stances, he prefigures the early rock and roll musician, whose beating back plays as "an intervention in the urban fashioning of the skin that joins flesh and stone."[46] I will return to the relation between rhythm and urban violence in the next chapter; here, I would begin to notice that, in an originary temporal twist, historical beating seems to have produced the conditions of possibility for the process of subject formation to which the backbeat responds. It is for this very reason—because the percussive field is posited as simultaneously structural and historical (which also means immersed in a convoluted temporality)—that other possibilities might be envisioned, in a creative incongruity between what grounds and what is grounded. "All syncopation . . . is caught up in the socio-genesis of the subject," writes Mowitt following Catherine Clément's reading of the mirror phase as a staging of the musical syncope in its pairing of dissonance and resolution.[47] Leaving aside doubts about Clément's orthopedic treatment of the imago, does this entail that all subject formation is caught up in syncopation? In other words, can we find the traces of a process that exceeds syncopation, of a rhythmic articulation that does not pivot around the beat?

I think of the work done by and through rhuthmos as less a substitution than a displacement of this percussive model, a way of disturbing its beat, of throwing off-balance the historical alliance of time and measure and the ways it has concurred to regulate the transformation of the subject. To the extent that it emerges as a disjointed, improper configuration, the rhythm of the aura intervenes in this tradition of regulated subjection, which is at once ontological and political, upsetting it as it blurs the very boundaries between subject and object, almost—but not quite—to the point of dissolution. In the case of cinema, this other rhythm would appear through the operations of montage, as they occur in the relationship between shots and in each shot's internal arrangement; it would cut across the distinction between the visual, the acoustic, and the haptic, bringing into play colors, sounds, and contours. Here cinema would be resisting or folding on itself the very formal principle (montage) that, in Benjamin's account, had prompted its development. In this respect, *Contempt* and *Mulholland Drive* can be said to enact a politics of memory that does not precede their formal—rhythmic—articulation but coincides with it (the relevance of their thematic interventions notwithstanding). In my reading,

I will concentrate on two brief sequences and claim them as "profane illuminations." As in the case of Surrealism, *flânerie,* and drug experiments, they confront us with *another* vision, a vision born on the side of things and their futural memory, in that unconscious encounter with the world that cinema, like Benjamin's writing, at once registers and performs.[48] It is in this realm of fugitive configurations that cinema can affirm itself as a medium of experience and, as such, a mode of political resistance in its own right.

YELLOW, RED, BLUE

The year is 1963 and *Contempt* opens with a shot of Godard's cinematographer, Raoul Coutard, operating a Mitchell camera in a semi-deserted lot of Cinecittà. Godard's voice-over recites the film credits and then adds, "'The cinema,' said André Bazin, 'substitutes for our look a world which conforms to our desires.' *Contempt* is the story of this world." A film suspended between documentary and fiction, *Contempt* proclaims cinema's immense power at the same time as it declares its imminent death. In the sequences that follow this self-reflexive beginning, *Contempt* will continue to foreground the workings of cinema, almost accounting for all the different phases of production and reception. As Laura Mulvey notices, *Contempt* offers us a "triptych" of settings in which the end of cinema is rehearsed "on location" and with remarkable characters: first the studio lot, where Paul (Michel Piccoli), a French screenwriter for hire, meets the uncouth American producer (Jack Palance) together with his multilingual assistant (Georgia Moll); then the projection room, where these three characters join the German director (Fritz Lang, playing himself) as he screens the rushes of his current adaptation of Homer's *Odyssey,* which is failing the producer's commercial expectations and is to be revised by Paul; and finally, a wall covered with peeling movie posters (Howard Hawk's *Hatari!,* Roberto Rossellini's *Vanina Vanini,* Alfred Hitchcock's *Psycho,* and Godard's own *Vivre sa vie*), in front of which Paul, his wife Camille (Brigitte Bardot), Lang, the producer, and his assistant all cross paths, anticipating the film's tragic finale as Camille leaves in the producer's speeding sports car.[49] Every image in this triptych presents a tightly woven texture of quotations from the domains of cinema, painting, literature, and poetry, to the point that the actors themselves, as Jacques Aumont observes, are "vehicles, in the flesh, of part of the past, of history. They are living quotations and, already, survivors of a vanished world."[50] But if Godard's aesthetics of quotation permeates the entire film (the love story of Paul and Camille develops as a modern reenactment of Odysseus and Penelope's vicissitudes, not to speak of Lang's role as a mythical filmmaker), it is the arrangement of the screening room sequence that most poignantly revives the conditions for an enigmatic encounter with the past.

The sequence intercuts shots of the characters with the rushes they are watching: images of plaster statues—Penelope, Athena, Poseidon, and other Greek gods—partially painted and filmed against the sky or an expanse of grass as if they were about to come to life; actual human figures, heavily made-up actors impersonating Penelope, Odysseus, and a slain suitor, respectively filmed against a yellow, red, and blue wall (the film's primary colors); and, finally, documentary-like images of a mermaid and Odysseus swimming in the Mediterranean Sea.[51] Yet what unfolds is more than a *mise-en-abyme* of spectatorship. The sequence resists being held, grasped from the viewpoint of a subject—it does not subsist as an intended temporal object, albeit one that has the power of informing its intentional counterpart, as Stiegler would suggest. Instead, its complex sensorial layering constitutes a knot that cannot be unraveled, that is loosened and tied again without ever dissolving or coalescing into a single shape. "Every soul is a rhythmic knot," writes Stéphane Mallarmé.[52] In *Contempt*, the soul that is "rhythmed" expands through the screen(s), the latter becoming less a barrier than a membrane through which "someone" is being composed and decomposed as always more than one. This is not the membrane of consciousness, Freud's callous envelope, against which recollection can occur, but a porous, vibrant membrane, an instrument that plays across or, rather, in the break of sensorial divisions.

Is Bardot a modern Penelope? Does she play Camille as the unwilling protagonist of a plot others have started to rewrite? Yellow, red, blue—this is as meaningful a plot as any other in *Contempt,* a weaving of colors that return in the painted eyes and lips of the statues as pellicles of seeing, and then in the walls behind the mythical characters, and on the grass dotted with poppies (Proust is never too far away). Another plot—the camera moving in toward Lang and then toward the first statue on screen and then around the second statue, as if Lang and the statues belonged to the same

FIGURE 8. *Contempt* (Jean-Luc Godard, 1963): the strife between line and color.

FIGURE 9. *Contempt* (Jean-Luc Godard, 1963): Penelope against a yellow background in Fritz Lang's adaptation of the *Odyssey*.

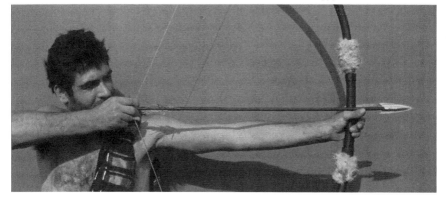

FIGURE 10. *Contempt* (Jean-Luc Godard, 1963): Odysseus against a red background in Lang's *Odyssey*.

world; not a shot-reverse shot but a superimposition of sorts, a muddling of the line connecting the eye to its object, the opening of a transversal dimension in the fabric of time. And yet another one—Georges Delerue's counter-punctual music, whose regular, broad gestures produce a sense of slow inexorability, a moving toward what is coming to us from the past. The musical rhythm would be predictable, measured in advance, if not for a cadence that remains unresolved over the image of the Neptune statue like an interrupted return; and for a jolt in the sonic space of the projection room, an omitted transition that abruptly takes us to the island of Capri, where the footage is being filmed—a prolonged caesura, an internal, constitutive reverberation, the echo of a subject that is always in more than one place and more than one time. There are other, smaller and yet critical disturbances: we hear the sound of waves as a mermaid swims off the island, while other similar shots are left silent, and at times Delerue's music serves as the diegetic sound of the image world we see. Such an intermixing of the diegetic and the extra-diegetic does not follow firm rules; rather, it seems to occur in response to a mood: not exactly the mood of the characters but something like the mood of the film itself—its rhuthmos, its disposition—as it is being composed for us, with us, in different sites at once.

Two decades before making *Scénario du film "Passion"* (1982) and appearing as a silhouette in front of a white screen, Godard conjures up the rhythm of a memory in the process of being created. I will call this memory *impersonal* because it emerges as a configuration that finds no stable reference point—not in the evanescent composition of the sequence, not in the characters, who already subsist at the crossings of multiple discursive histories, and even less in the spectators. Simultaneously inside and outside the film(s), we find ourselves arranged, configured in the texture of a memory that does not belong to us and yet becomes ours—a memory that *pictures* us, transforms us into moving pictures; not self-identical and self-present images but transitory configurations, echoes of images, if you will. The world of dreams is not far off. In the Baudelaire essay, Benjamin cites Paul Valéry on the decentering aspects of oneiric perception: "To say, 'Here I see such and such an object' does not establish an equation between me and the object.... In dreams, however, there is such an equation. The things I see, see me just as much as I see them."[53] Godard's cinema translates this porosity, this reversibility of passivity and activity through the rhythm of its editing so that bodies do not end at the skin. But what it performs for us (with us) is other than the fantasy or impossible memory of the undifferentiated. As the apparition of a distance that is at once spatial and temporal, the scene's aura returns us to the process of differentiation through which we become subjects, opening up the possibility for other modes of being to emerge, other articulations of experience to be glimpsed and pursued.

We discover a similar ambiguity in Benjamin's early text "The Rainbow: A Dialogue on Fantasy," where the dream of pure color—color as "pure seeing"—recounted by Margarethe contrasts with the account of painting offered in response by her painter friend Georg. Painting, he explains, springs not from color but from form, from the marking of a surface, and is thus unable to effectively render the chromatic immersion we experience in dreams or during the early years of childhood. Indeed, while describing her dream, Margarethe says, "I was not a viewer, I was only viewing. And what I saw were not things . . . [but] only colors. And I myself was colored in this landscape." If there is a subject in this experience, it seems to be color itself or, rather, a seeingness that folds on itself and, in the process, generates chromatic variations of which the dreamer is but one. "Perception . . . is itself dispersed [*zerstreut*] in color," Benjamin will add later in the text.[54] That is, perception occurs amid a field of indefinite gradations, rather than in relation to a surface that serves as background for a clear-cut figure. In *The Colour of Experience,* Howard Caygill shows that, already at this early stage, Benjamin is undertaking a revision of Kantian philosophy's distinction between understanding and intuition and, in particular, developing a critique of the concept of form. For Benjamin, the inscription of the line on a surface constitutes but a particular case of what he calls a "configuration," a patterning of experience that (speculatively) exceeds the distinction between subject and object and, concomitantly, that between form and matter. In the dialogue on color, the distinction between subject and object dissolves more radically than in Valéry's portrayal of the dream, yet here, too, there remains some differentiation—one that pertains to color rather than form—and, together with it, the promise of "a new chromatic articulation of experience."[55]

In *Contempt,* the auratic coincides with the rediscovery of rhythm as precarious, intermittent modulation of the sensible (rhuthmos). Rather than coalescing into a monumental present, the projection room sequence unfolds as the trace of a past that has repeatedly been transformed, a time that never existed fully and is thus open to receive the contingencies of the future. In the artwork essay, Benjamin refers to Able Gance, proclaiming, "Shakespeare, Rembrandt, Beethoven will make films."[56] Caygill suggests that we relate the Abel Gance quotation to Benjamin's conception of the artwork as permeable and capable of including (both retrospectively and in a gesture of anticipation) the possibilities that the future will have realized, including the "possibility of their becoming films."[57] Indeed, while following Romanticism's method of immanent critique and experimenting with the artwork as a field of possibilities, Benjamin comes to redefine the very notion of "origin" in accordance with his speculative concept of experience. In the epistemo-critical prologue to *The Origin of German Tragic Drama*, Benjamin writes:

> The term origin is not intended to describe the process by which the existent came into being, but rather to describe that which emerges in the process of becoming and disappearance. Origin is an eddy in the stream of the becoming, and in its rhythmic movement it swallows the material involved in the process of genesis.[58]

In commenting on the passage, Caygill emphasizes how such a stance subtracts the notion of origin from a rigid ordering of time and space: rather than constituting a static point, origin forms a rhythmic patterning, a configuration that exists in intermittence, coming into and withdrawing from appearance. Concomitantly, for Benjamin, method as "digression," as a "continual pausing for breath," as a mode of encounter with the artwork that follows an "irregular rhythm," cannot but be the most appropriate for this tracing of origins. In the projection room sequence, and in attunement with this method, the auratic emerges not as the stronghold of an unmovable tradition but, rather, as an erratic memory formation, an articulation of the sensible that reinvents the origin of the *Odyssey*, enabling the past to look back *toward* us.

NO-ONE IS BREATHING

What persists in *Contempt* and reappears in *Mulholland Drive* is this solicitation of a distance, a non-coincidence in space and time that prevents the past from being closed off, relegated to the domain of "what happened," deprived of memory's powers of creation. A historical phenomenon, the auratic reconfigures itself in relation to mutated conditions of production and reception. "Made in Hollywood" in the decisive decade of transition between analog and digital reproduction, and about a hundred years after the Lumière brothers' first screening, *Mulholland Drive* leads us through a city almost empty of crowds. Unlike Baudelaire's Paris or Poe's London, the city that Lynch sets out to explore has retreated into the enclosures of the car and the private home, with only sporadic venues for collective gathering—most notably the Club Silencio, a former movie palace and now the site of mysterious performances by an emcee who proclaims, "*No hay banda*, and yet we hear a band. It's all recorded," and a singer who passionately lip-syncs Roy Orbison's "Crying." It is here, halfway through the film, that Betty/Diane (Naomi Watts) and Rita/Camilla (Laura Harring) plunge into a vortex that undoes their identities and puts an end to their blissful love story. The first and second halves of *Mulholland Drive* are often interpreted in light of a straightforward distinction between reality and imagination. After the stint at the Club Silencio, the two women disappear from each other's lives, only to reappear in a reversed guise: Watts is no longer the naïve and talented newcomer to Los Angeles, whose arresting audition represents a first step toward stardom, but is now a hopeless victim of the Hollywood machine; and Harring, no longer the beautiful amnesic who falls in love with Watts as they search together for her forgotten identity, has become instead a manipulative film star, whose cruelty toward Watts is only heightened by Watts's obsessive desire. For the film to "make sense," many critics have argued, the first half needs to be retroactively interpreted as Watts's fantasy, the wishful reimagining of her life as she is about to kill herself in despair. On her deathbed, Watts dreams about what simply never happened. Against this domesticating approach, I propose that we focus on the opening montage sequence and the gaps it opens in the temporal fabric of the film.

Everything we might expect from an homage to Frank Tashlin's *The Girl Can't Help It* (1956) seems to be in place: young dancers moving joyfully against a fluorescent background, their bodies being doubled and even tripled as they cross paths and are superimposed onto one another; all the while, the beat of the jitterbug dance is primed, the syncopation throwing us off just a bit, in what Adorno would call the illusion of the unruly, or "false rhythm."[59] In a veritable resurfacing of the old cinema of attractions, it is as if these images displayed themselves for us, reaching out, *almost* touching the pellicles of our eyes and yet also remaining inapprehensible in their kinetic virtuosity. That this repeated intimation of touch does not turn into a striking or a fully realized percussive event will prove to be less reassuring than puzzling. What Angela McRobie calls "the possibility of being at once *there* and *not there*"—the intermittence produced by the material conditions of the dance hall or disco (darkness, crowdedness, often "trancelike" rhythms)—furtively turns into the im-possibility of being neither here nor there.[60] Something feels askew, and soon we cannot ignore the low rumble subtending the dance scene, like the echo of a subterranean world that has begun to tremble, to move up toward the surface. It is Angelo Badalamenti's signature sound, synthesized strings muddying the texture of the jazz piece. We also hear a crowd noise, coming from far away, perhaps the sound of a live performance.

By the time Watts's radiant face appears on the screen together with the suggestion of a story line (she is in the limelight, being applauded), the atmospheric rumbling and the distant crowd sounds have precipitated a sense of uneasiness, while the couples multiplying against a background that has no depth start feeling like insects crawling up from the same underground world. The audiovisual layering produces a fissure, a discrepancy that brings us into a scene where there is no comfortable space for us—a scene that is too flat, that proliferates from within, so that we, too, find ourselves crawling out of it, together with the dancers and the girl and the demonic old couple. Until we enter a claustrophobic space, the camera getting closer and closer to an empty pillow and sheets the color of congealed blood, the soundtrack registering somebody's heavy breathing, like an exhaustion of the heartbeat. But this transition to the bedroom space, which would constitute an abrupt interruption if not for a brief superimposition connecting the two scenes, does not allow us to gather, to collect ourselves after the scattering experience of the dance. On the contrary, the point-of-view shot further disturbs our sense of corporeal boundaries, as if there were "no-one" here where somebody is breathing. Without a sharp cut, the interruption of the dance scene continues to linger—as a delayed interruption—in the bedroom scene. Indeed, the two form one heterogeneous sequence.

In a film punctuated by all sorts of hallucinatory images, nothing but our desire to anchor ourselves in space and time confirms that the bedroom shots should be given priority over the dancing sequence. If the forms of another, perhaps happier, life are to be traced back to the bedroom where somebody is about to die, I suggest that we relate to them as images of involuntary memory rather than sheer imagination. Regarding involuntary memory, Benjamin writes:

> Not only do its images not come when we try to call them up ... they are images which we have never seen before we remember them. This is most clearly the case in those images in which—like in some dreams—we see ourselves. We stand in front of ourselves, the way we might have stood somewhere in a prehistoric past, but never before our waking gaze.

In moments of extreme danger or impending death, we are seized by the decentering vision of ourselves as we might have appeared to an alien gaze, in a time before chronology—as someone that is *almost* out of reach or, in Lynch's universe, that exists in an alternative, simultaneous life. Here, Hansen would remark, the auratic reveals its affinity with the uncanny, becoming the conduit for another kind of shock, one that possesses the ability to revive unconscious memories and immerse us in an outlandish world. These images, Benjamin continues, "flash by in as rapid a sequence as the booklets of our childhood, precursors of the cinema, in which we admired a boxer, a swimmer or a tennis player."[61] As hands and eyes join in an exhilarating simulation of automatism, what we witness is almost a rehearsal of cinema's powers as a technology of the spectral. *Mulholland Drive*'s opening sequence produces such a limit-experience, leaving us suspended in a moment of impossible recognition, as we are looked at by a picture of ourselves that we have never seen.

But in this composite scene, we witness an even more disturbing recurrence. What haunts us most sharply is not an image or sound but, rather, a fissure between images and sounds, an internal disjunction whose effect will resonate throughout the film. Such a discontinuity will become conspicuous in the lip-syncing scene at the Club Silencio, when the singer's recorded voice continues to play after the singer faints and is carried off stage; it is in the opening sequence, however, that it is first activated. In "The Echo of the Subject," Lacoue-Labarthe pauses on Reik's description of a somehow similar scene: it is the middle of the night and people are dancing in a bright dance hall; the spectator is standing close enough to see them but not to hear the music. "The rhythm clue is missing," Reik writes, and Lacoue-Labarthe insists on the malaise produced by this phantomlike arrangement, one in which repetition becomes unhinged in the experience of an impossible doubling of the visual and the acoustic.[62] In this passage, rhythm still belongs to the musical register, and Lacoue-Labarthe will soon push Reik's theoretical boundaries. What remains relevant for our reading of *Mulholland Drive* is that Reik's uncanny scene appears as irrevocably split or, rather, folded across a coincidence (of sound and vision) that radically evades us. Indeed, the most haunting sequences in *Mulholland Drive* are those oversaturated scenes in which similarly "nothing occurs," if not the return of this discrepancy, like a synchronization that has already gone amiss. If rhythm can be considered as the "condition of possibility for the subject," it is because it is operative below or beyond the division of the visible and the audible.[63] "In the beginning, rhythm, says von Bülow"—which means that it begins with what has no simple beginning: rhythm as repetition, self-differentiation, spacing.[64] We are "rhythmed," composed and decomposed (not unlike Gustav Mahler) by a rhythm that eludes the theoretical because it emerges precisely where the theoretical constitutes itself.[65]

In both *Mulholland Drive* and *Contempt,* the auratic as rhythmic configuration affirms itself as a time of protracted interruptions and forgotten beginnings. By producing a discrepancy, even a jolt, in the relation between temporal dimensions, it enables us to glimpse modes of experience that reach through the skin of the specular image, the boundaries of a subject perpetually wrestling with its bodily ego.[66] In these films, the auratic returns as the immeasurable interval that prevents the past from being closed off and privatized, relegated to the domain of "what happened" (to *me* or *us*), deprived of memory's powers of reinvention: it is through the auratic that we are remembered and reinvented as others than ourselves. If, as Stiegler claims, art seeks to temporalize *differently,* I will remark that it fulfills this function not by identifying subjects of consciousness (those who are "missing" in our hyperindustrial times) but by turning both subject and object into erratic formations, arrangements of a discontinuous and impersonal memory.[67] The heartbeat of montage belongs to a subjectivity that is articulated in its very intermittent dispersion—a fabric or mesh that repeats and interrupts the rhythms of a past that does not coalesce. More and less than a beat, eccentric and irregular, the heartbeat of *Contempt* and *Mulholland Drive* belongs to no-one.

CODA

"Silenzio, si gira! Silenzio!" ("Quiet, we're rolling! Quiet!") are among the last words we hear in *Contempt*, shouted by a crew member as Fritz Lang is about to film the last scene of his *Odyssey* atop Curzio Malaparte's modernist villa. Lang's slow tracking shot frames the Greek hero casting his first look on the island of Ithaca, while Godard's slightly faster camera movement leaves him behind, offering us just an image of the sea. In *Le Livre d'image* (*The Image Book*, 2018), Godard's latest essay film, we hear these words almost at the end—a coda is still awaiting us—over a black background and the list of texts, films, and musical pieces that the filmmaker has once again edited together in an operation of radical montage. But if Godard had previously experimented with superimposition, slow motion, image freeze, flickering, et cetera in *Histoire(s) du cinéma*, here these techniques, which never amounted to a repertoire, are adopted with a new kind of abandonment, a readiness to shed one's own forms: the forms of the films he has loved and those he has made, together with the form of his own self. The latter had already undergone a process of divestiture in a number of works, yet what we witness in *The Image Book* is a metamorphosis that leaves few recognizable traces of the physical and figurative body *(corpus)* of the filmmaker as he endures the end of his life and career, not to speak of the death of cinema. This metamorphosis occurs by means of color—color redistributing itself within and across the outlines of things, splashing out, washing over, bleeding through, having no other end than its own becoming. It is the return of auratic memory as forgetting according to color, unpredictable and relentless. Among the images that most notably bear this process we find the close-ups of a film strip, unfurling or already stretched out, less a thing than a color patch made of color patches; then myriads of trains, stripes of color rushing nowhere or to hell, and flowers, Rainer Maria Rilke's "flowers between the rails" together with Marcel Proust's poppies; and, above all, images of water.[68]

In her review for *Artforum*, brilliantly titled "Sync or Swim," Amy Taubin notices that even images that already appear in *Histoire(s)* are "made new through the relationship of the eye and the hand that turns the dials on the digital board or that fingers the digital paintbrush and the touch screen."[69] What interests me in Taubin's comments on digital coloring is the detection of a mutation in the technicity of the body, like when André Bazin describes the Bell and Howell 16mm camera as "a projection of hand and eye, almost a living part of the operator, instantly in tune with his awareness."[70] For Godard, Rimbaud's "century of hands" has not quite passed, and he proclaims this new film to be the work of "five digits, five senses, five continents." However, unlike Taubin, I interpret Godard's digital expansion as the attempt not to produce "a film that could be as handmade as a painting"[71] but to let his hands become part of a fluttering prosthetic body, a body that is incessantly bordering out of itself by means of color or, rather, *as* color. To declare, as Godard's voice-over does, that human beings are defined by their capacity "to think with their hands" already means to consider them as inherently prosthetic, indissociable from a technics that has always been "inventive as well as invented."[72] (Even the hand that opens the film, a detail from Leonardo Da Vinci's last painting, *St. John the Baptist,* appears in a heavily xeroxed version.) The question then seems to become, what can a hand *made of* digital color, a hand that is color amid colors, do? Can it think a form that overflows the edges of the line, can it turn color lines into chromatic configurations of which it is itself part? I return to the question of color at the end of this chapter on auratic memory to situate it more directly in relation to the covert anxieties, if not overt fears about race and sexual difference, that Godard's film essay exposes and transmutes. In *Chromophobia,* David Batchelor points us in this direction when he underscores that the "purging of colour" in Western art and culture, its subordination to the purity or clarity of the line, has been traditionally implemented in two ways:

> In the first, colour is made out to be the property of some "foreign" body—usually the feminine, the oriental, the primitive, the infantile, the vulgar, the queer or the pathological. In the second, colour is relegated to the realm of the superficial, the supplementary, the inessential or the cosmetic.[73]

These two modes often work together in a conflation of "the sinister and the superficial" that is the mark of "prejudice."[74] In *The Image Book,* the question of color reaches beyond the crucial thematic attention that Godard, here and elsewhere, devotes to the history of warfare and colonization and, in particular, to the relationship between Europe and the Middle East; it also reaches beyond the question of representation (accurate or nuanced versus stereotypical), uncovering the latter as a way of domesticating color's ontological force.

When it returns, in *The Image Book*'s many seascapes, the sea of *Contempt* has changed its color. Or, rather, the films' saturated primary colors— yellow, red, blue—have uncontrollably bled into the landscape, reworking the relationship between water, sky, rocks, and human beings. "Claudel has a phrase saying that a certain blue of the sea is so blue that only blood would be more red," writes Maurice Merleau-Ponty in *The Visible and the Invisible*, a book whose "intertwinings" Godard has often retraced. Merleau-Ponty refers to Claudel in a long, startling paragraph as he attempts to release color—this red, for instance—from its identity as a quale and affirms it as "a certain differentiation, an ephemeral modulation of this world—less a color or a thing, therefore, than a difference between things and colors, a momentary crystallization of colored being or of visibility." In a stylistic tour de force, Merleau-Ponty weaves this red into mutable constellations of other reds, claims its being "bound up" with things of different texture and shape, and foregrounds its being "literally not the same" in each case. But what Claudel's phrase intimates is something that Merleau-Ponty cannot quite say directly—that the blue of the sea is already different from itself; that "the tissue that lines [the alleged colors and visibles]," the flesh of the world, is dehiscence, non-coincidence, indefinite productivity.[75] As I mentioned in the introduction and argued in my previous book, I interpret the notion of flesh in this manner, dis-activating its pull toward coalescence, in light of Merleau-Ponty's own philosophical style, his incessant sliding from metaphor to metaphor, his thinking on the verge of the literal. Godard, too, privileges metonymy and here he moves (us) from seascape to seascape, from color wave to color wave. But he goes even further: if Merleau-Ponty's description of color constellations remains on the side of the seen (which is other than an object), Godard extends it or, rather, folds it onto the side of the seer (which is other than a subject), according to Merleau-Ponty's own principle of reversibility. Indeed, in the passage following the one on color, Merleau-Ponty writes of the seer as a being that is inextricably of vision and touch; more specifically, he speaks of hands touching each other and the world to which they belong, not in order to explain vision by analogy, but to show that the look is already a "palpation of the eye."[76] Godard performs this reversibility between the seer and the seen, turning his hands into a constellation of feverish colors.

There seems to be a privileged relationship between this upsurge of color and the deep memory of water or, as Bachelard would say, the memory of deep water, although here we find not matter but a force field of fluctuating forms *(rhuthmoi)*, configurations of color that undo the power of lines and abstract color divisions. Water is the water of the Po Delta, in Rossellini's *Paisan* (1946), where Italian resistance fighters are drowned by the Nazis; of a nondescript port, on an Arabic language TV channel, as masked men holding a religious banner execute and throw their prisoners down the platform; of the San Francisco Bay, in *Vertigo* (1958), where Judy/Madeleine is rescued by Scottie; and of the river canal, in *L'Atalante* (1934), where Jean and Juliette's images swim together in a dance of atoms. Godard's intervention is most conspicuous in *Vertigo*, with its meddling greens and blues, and the news footage, where the sea turns crimson and magenta, and yet the black-and-white scenes, too, are altered, as grays, blacks, and whites reclaim their existence as concrete colors rather than gradations on a scale of abstraction. At the same time, the sound of water acquires sculptural relief, whether intermingling with voices or reverberating by itself. Later, in the section titled "La Région Centrale" ("The Central Region")—an homage to Michael Snow's homonymous film that reinvents the duration of the latter—this history of water becomes more overtly the history of colonization and orientalism, as Godard focuses on the Middle East and the violence that it has suffered "sous les yeux de l'Occident" ("under Western eyes"), including the violence of representation.[77] Now the sea waves are dense blue, their foamy crests and the sky yellow, at times almost acid yellow; shortly afterward, both sea and sky are of a bright darker red; then yellow and red return to encompass the screen when a bomb detonates, one of the many explosions that the film paints in blasts of color, almost fireworks, pushing war's spectacular economy to its limits; and then blue, blue water, blue smoke. Unlike Le Corbusier in *Journey to the East*, Godard does not retreat into whiteness, pure or generalized whiteness, but plunges into color, exploring it through a tumultuous labor of differentiation.[78] This is not a compensatory move, an attempt at making good a history that is now behind us; hope endures to the very extent that destruction is also enduring and the sea that we see also carries the images of those who remain largely invisible, those who cross it at peril or drown amid its waves. Godard's most daring gesture is not to expose the exotic, "the sinister and the superficial" of representation but to turn a history of violence in which color has been dried up and deployed as a category for classification and conquest into a futural memory of colors, of other colors and ways of releasing the potential of the sensible world.

More radically than *Contempt*, *The Image Book* transforms memory into an experience of chromatic re-embodiment, a reinvention of spectatorship that possesses ontological force. As I replay the film on my laptop, I am captivated rather than disturbed by the sunlight filtering though the shades and the color effects it produces on the glass desk. If I have always believed that darkness is to the film viewer what water is to the swimmer, now I find my hands vibrating in this pool of colors, as if we (my body, the desk, the film) were part of some oddly shaped and volatile chromatic configuration—as if it were colors watching other colors. To the very extent that it enacts this color-seeingness without congealing or exhausting it, Godard's proposal for an ontology of color exceeds the "ontology of bodies" that Jean-Luc Nancy offers us in *Being Singular Plural*. Nancy's "we," the "we" of our originary co-existence as co-appearance, is other than a juxtaposition of parts or a totality and yet it still coincides with the distinct volume of bodies. It is true that these bodies exist each moment only in their multiple states and intersections and that a body is "every body," "whether made of stone, wood, plastic, or flesh."[79] But these bodies remain contoured and even "impenetrable" in their "being plural singular." What Godard lets us see instead is the possibility for configurations to emerge that cut across or, rather, fold in and out of all sort of bodies—arrangements that are radically heterogeneous in interspersing the human and the animal, the animal and the vegetal, the animate and the inanimate, and so on. Saying, as Nancy does, that "I would no longer be a 'human' if I did not have this exteriority 'in me,' in the form of the quasi-minerality of bone" is not quite like saying that what is *intermittently* on and around this screen is a configuration of colors made of celluloid and flesh and bone and glass.[80] In Godard's cinema, as in Resnais's *Mon oncle d'Amérique,* a "singularity" is less a body than an idiosyncratic configuration of matter (rhuthmos). That it does not need to follow a beat (that beating to which even Nancy still pays tribute) stands among the philosophical contributions of modern cinema.

Remembering according to form is exhausting, and so is remembering otherwise. At the end of the post-credits coda, the dandy from Max Ophuls's *Le Plaisir* (1952), a mask covering his aged face, throws himself into a frenzied dance, until he collapses onto the floor. It is a mute or silent dance, its joyful desperation rendered all the more touching by the overblown whites bleeding out of their contours, as if they, too, were jolting out of their skin. Earlier in the film, we clung to the less conspicuously altered sequences (above all, the interminable tracking shot from Jacques Tourneur's *Berlin Express* [1948]) as surviving tokens of a world that is sinking or exploding into color. Later on, we began to look at them as something curious that had been artificially compacted or synthesized by willful, repetitive coding. Now, we see this uncut scene as something outright strange, uncanny to the extent that it returns to us as a demand—the demand that life makes of us, to be lived in all its modes. In its frenzy, what the scene shows is its potential to become other or, rather, it shows that this potential had been there all along, restrained and yet not vanquished by the *mise-en-forme* of narrative cinema and our viewing habits. But this end does not quite end, in spite of all, as Godard's auratic memory, his forgetting by means of color is (pace Agamben) perceptual re-creation and not only de-creation of the world.[81]

4. Medium

HISTORIES OF ENCLOSURE

Sitting in the corner room of his Moscow apartment sometime after the end of War World II, Sergei Eisenstein observes the landscape outside its windows:

> Another window looks out on an empty field.
> This field was once an apple orchard.
> I dug up the apple orchard—
> in 1938.[1]

What he sees (a village from one window, an empty field from the other) is a site marked by a history of struggle, a sequence of violent confrontations between Russian fighters and foreign invaders: Napoleon in the nineteenth century, the Germans as late as 1941, and the Teutonic Knights of the Holy Roman Empire as early as the thirteenth century. Indeed, the historic Battle of the Ice occurred here only in Eisenstein's own *Алекса́ндр Не́вский* (*Alexander Nevskyi*, 1938), as the director uprooted an apple orchard to make room for the ice-covered battlefield; the empty field is all that ostensibly remains. Now, sitting in this sunlit room, Eisenstein is about to execute another radical overturning of space, this time by virtue of a most active kind of viewing. On the wall between the two windows hangs an early etching by Piranesi, called *Carcere oscura (Dark Prison)*, which had fascinated him for years. A calm, even lyrical composition, *Carcere oscura* appears to be only a distant precursor of the convulsing architectural visions found in the later *Carceri d'invenzione (Imaginary Prisons)* and used by Thomas De Quincey to describe his opium-induced hallucinations—unless, that is, we "set it in motion," as Eisenstein does, bringing about an "ecstatic effect" that leaves no element of the composition untouched. "I ponder over what would happen to this etching," he writes, "if it were brought to a state of ecstasy, if it were brought outside of itself."[2] Like in the case of El Greco, Eisenstein conceives of this experiment as an "explosion," a dynamic and, in fact, violent "transfiguration" of the picture's lines, surfaces, and volumes. In the process, a new picture takes hold of our eyes, "a whirlwind, as in a hurricane, dashing in all directions: ropes, runway staircases, exploding arches, stone blocks breaking away from each other."[3] Here, precipitating "forward" and receding "into the depths" are all but the same, in a madness of vision that shatters the contours of the objects, but not their concreteness.

Eisenstein's critical operation, which develops through an irregularly cadenced prose, does not emerge ex nihilo. In contrast, it turns out to be doubly bounded, pushed and pulled, if you will, by preexisting dynamics. On the one hand, the original etching already possesses a "tendency to explode," to leap out of itself, as it presents the viewer with a dissolution of forms and means of expression that upsets its own internal structure.[4] A latent motion pervades the composition and sets the stage for the frenzied "rebellion of the objects" that Eisenstein's intervention will precipitate.[5] On the other hand, next to *Carcere oscura* hangs a second etching, also by Piranesi, but belonging to the later *Carceri*. We can surmise that, in its feverish fragmentation, this other etching has presented Eisenstein with both the inspiration and the validation for his experiment. As a result, we are now faced not by a series of discreet, autonomous pictures but by a sequence of shots. In "The Historicity of the Avant-Garde: Piranesi and Eisenstein," Manfredo Tafuri rightly observes that there exists a profound agreement between Eisenstein's method of ecstatic criticism and his theory of montage. For Eisenstein, "montage is the stage of the *explosion of the shot*," an explosion that is to occur when the shot's internal tension reaches its apex.[6] Tafuri interprets the reading of Piranesi as the director's attempt to strike a compromise between the disintegration of forms and the preservation of figurative values, fragmentation, and organic unity—the avant-garde and realism. While attending to the complexity and internal division of Eisenstein's thought, Luka Arsenjuk speaks of a "figure-in-crisis" and, more specifically, of an originary self-division, "the fact that the figure is in its unity already something divided, at odds with itself."[7] Like in the drawing of the barricade from "Montage 1937," dynamization proves crucial in "deforming and animating the figure," thus leading to a release of perception from habit.[8] If unity remains the final objective of Eisenstein's cinema, it is important to acknowledge that such unity is aimed at and reached only by virtue of a dialectic of division.

Rhythm plays a multifaceted role in this respect. On the one hand, it unwinds the iconic dimension of the picture, its relationships of resemblance, introducing a play of forces whose primary medium is time rather than space. On the other hand, it does all this on behalf of symbolization, the production of an essential meaning, ultimately fulfilling the demands of synthesis.[9] In the Piranesi essay, essential to the compromise between multiplicity and unity is the drive to hold the frame in place—its function, its value—amid repeated explosions and, concomitantly, to maintain a unitary viewpoint—a communion of affect, thought, and action—amid shifting perspectives. As reconstituted in "Montage and Architecture," the Athenian Acropolis provides its visitors with a "montage plan," a route to be followed step by step; conversely, the montage sequence functions as a "path" that is shared by both director and spectator.[10] In "Laocoön" and "[Rhythm]," Eisenstein identifies rhythm as the fundamental means for binding a sequence's disparate elements into a whole and, more specifically, for accomplishing that generalization of the theme without which cinema remains a medium of depiction, adequate for stories but not for ideas.[11] Sound plays a new decisive role in this respect, and yet, well before Edmund Meisel composed the score for Броненóсец «Потёмкин» (*The Battleship Potemkin*, 1925), the film had already given expression to a tension that reached beyond the plot while remaining integral to it. Potemkin's bare rhythm "was not a generalisation of the rhythm of the ship's engines; it was a generalised image of the collective heartbeat of the battleship's crew, for which the engines themselves were a *visual* generalising image."[12] It is through the rhythm of montage that cinema is able to produce generalization without abstraction, thus ensuring the persistence of a viewpoint that has the power of a communal heartbeat. For Eisenstein, rhythm is nothing less than the aesthetic condition for a revolutionary articulation of the image and the achievement of a new unity. Almost a century later, the question of rhythm's political function, which first imposed itself with the choral art of Plato's polis, acquires renewed urgency: how can we envision a rhythm that sets place in motion, rediscovering its memory and potential, while also eschewing a recuperation of unity and identity—a rhythm that expresses what Paolo Virno has called the "mode of being of the many," the multitude rather than the people?[13]

I sit in front of Victor Burgin's digital loop *Prairie* (2015), a silent projection piece, the day after it opens at the University of Chicago, about four miles from the site that it chose to investigate: now occupied by Mies van der Rohe's Crown Hall building at the Illinois Institute of Technology, the plot of land at the intersection of Thirty-Fourth and State had seen the flourishing of the Mecca apartment building—the city's most vital center of African American culture, demolished in order to make room for the modernist masterpiece in the 1950s—and, decades earlier, the arrival of white settlers. The text accompanying the exhibition states that, like Burgin's other recent works, "*Prairie* responds to specific architectural sites . . . and explores erased or disappeared cultural histories, real and/ or imagined, inscribed in the built environment."[14] Indeed, *Prairie* places Chicago's fraught history of urban planning and its cartographic ambitions within the larger framework of colonial expansion (the marking out of global lines), while also attending to the world-making function of what might seem most private—*fantasy*. In its psychoanalytic sense, the latter is a "scene" or, rather, a "script" that stages the subject's desire through a series of overlays, spatial superimpositions that deeply trouble our sense of chronological succession.[15] After a few viewings, I recall Eisenstein's essay on Piranesi and wonder if Burgin somehow remembered it while looking at the site of which *Prairie* constitutes the complex trace. The reasons for such an association are certainly not missing: both pieces explore the intimate relationship existing between architecture and cinema, stillness and motion, simultaneity and succession. Yet, it is the difference, the distance separating them, that exercises the strongest power of attraction: rhythm is this difference, and my attention is absorbed by it. As *Prairie* unfurls, unfolds itself in a time of uncertain duration (eight minutes representing only its technical "length"), I encounter a rhythm whose function is more elusive and yet more troubling to the stability of both frame and point of view—perhaps a different kind of rhythm altogether. In Eisenstein, rhythm plays a distinctive role in aggregating perceptual forms under an internally split and yet unitary vision. On the other hand, in Burgin, rhythm emerges as a horizontal, recursive sliding of forms: a configuration that cannot stop undoing itself while attaining its singularity.

In this chapter, I would like to activate the notion of *rhuthmos* as a manner of flowing to explore the question of the frame in relation to the tracing of boundary lines. That is, I would like to situate this inquiry on rhythm in the context of a wider discussion on borders, in particular what Sandro Mezzadra and Brett Nielsen call "internal borders," less lines of clear demarcation than "complex patterns of spatial segregation that work to manage and rule populations marked by poverty, destitution, and often racial discrimination."[16] In this respect, the French *banlieues*, which Étienne Balibar describes as "a periphery at the very center of the great metropolitan areas" and connects to South African townships, present us with a composite example: here race and class act on each other to constitute "those who occupy it as eternally *displaced (out of place)* persons, the *internally excluded.*"[17] Mezzadra and Nielsen emphasize how Balibar's phrase, by interlocking the expressions "eternally" and "out of place," effectively points to a production of subjectivity that occurs through operations of both spatial and temporal bordering. Internal borders are also temporal in two crucial ways: they generate "zones of temporal suspension" or indefinite awaiting, a halt in the progression of clock time and narratives of social mobility; and they coincide with a repression of France's colonial past and its resurgence in contemporary migration policies, as Achille Mbembe argues in "The Republic and Its Beast," which was published during the 2005 riots.[18] But, if the *banlieues* possess an irreducible historical specificity, the logic of temporal bordering that has concurred to shape them emerged within the global context of primitive accumulation and colonialism; it is thus not surprising to find it at work in the segregated neighborhoods of North American cities, where memories of the Great Migration, slavery, and settler colonialism are kept in check by narratives of urban development, among others.[19] It is this logic that Burgin discreetly disrupts, displaces through a rhythm that deliberately fails to recompose space and time in a moment of synthesis.

To the extent that it revolves around the tracing of boundary lines, the definition of *enclosure* cannot but elude the capture of systematic thought. As Étienne Balibar underscores, "To mark out a border is, precisely, to define a territory, to delimit it, and so to register the identity of that territory, or confer one upon it. Conversely, however, to define or identify in general is nothing other than to trace a border, to assign boundaries or borders."[20] Border and definition are mutually implicated, dependent on each other in a circularity that frustrates strictly methodical thinking, while opening up the possibility of other modes of theoretical elaboration. It is at this juncture that I return to Roland Barthes's *How to Live Together*, the published notes for a lecture course at the Collège de France (1976–77), which specifically addresses the drawing of aesthetic boundaries. The course is devoted to exploring "idiorrhythmy" as the fantasy of a life lived with others and yet according to one's own rhythm—a fantasy that will upset our received notions of form, rhythm, and commonality as they emerge in both literature and life. To pursue this inquiry, Barthes mobilizes Friedrich Nietzsche's distinction between method and culture as "training" *(paideia)*: if method "fetishize[s] the goal as a privileged place, to the detriment of other possible places," culture proceeds along the "eccentric path of possibilities, stumbling among blocks of knowledge."[21] The resulting journey takes us from accounts of the *diaita* (diet, lifestyle) of early monastic clusters to Daniel Defoe's *Robinson Crusoe* and Émile Zola's *Pot Luck*, as Barthes attempts to trace the irregular, transitory, and yet distinctive contours of a life that resists the imposition of a rule, in the double sense of regulation and measuring instrument. The notion of rhuthmos, which intermittently appears throughout the lecture course, proves critical in this respect. Barthes explicitly contrasts the production of enclosures—from the partitioning of land to the demarcation of aesthetic frames—with the work done by rhuthmos or, rather, by the fantasy of rhuthmos as a "subtle" and idiosyncratic form: a modulation of space and time that remains irreducible, that cannot be translated according to a logic of equivalence.

I will return to Barthes's work as I claim for *Prairie* what at first might seem puzzling: its coming into view as a place where images of the past "live together" in a plural, nonhierarchical, provisional arrangement—a configuration that displays the contingent and fugitive character of rhuthmos. While repeatedly pointing to the violence of the history it reveals, the piece does not restage a fantasy of aggression and defense (a beating fantasy, if you will) but, rather, one of cohabitation at a distance. In what feels like a prolonged suspension of the beat, violence does not erupt and does not subside: it endures, as the piece's discreet rhythm prevents it from being played out and left behind, relegated to a previous historical phase. My second proposition, intimately connected to the first, is that this idiorrhythmic place is a photographic one: that it belongs to photography as an "expanding field," to borrow Peter Osborne's formulation, rather than narrative cinema.[22] In other words, I suggest that we conceive of *Prairie* as a singular photograph—a photograph that plays out its own rhythm. Several of the questions that I will be pursuing in this chapter revolve around such a seemingly impossible coincidence between photography and rhythm. I call it impossible to the extent that photography is traditionally regarded as the medium of instantaneity, whereas rhythm is most closely associated with music and its regulated duration. I will show that Burgin's projection piece reworks this very incongruence, leading to the reinvention of *photography as rhythm*—at once the mutation of a practice and the redefinition of the medium's conditions of intelligibility. Finally, in order to dispel the impression that I am merely trying to mark out new mediatic boundaries, I will focus on the last sequence in Michelangelo Antonioni's *L'Eclisse* (*The Eclipse*, 1962) and propose that we read it as a place of imperfect, self-differing simultaneity: a simultaneity in succession that opens up time's ultimate enclosure, the instant or now-point, and rewrites cinema's narrative history.

It is worth noticing that Barthes sets us on the trail of this other rhythm ahead of *How to Live Together* and its analysis of literary texts. In fact, he does so in the context of an image critique that focuses on Eisenstein's construction of space and time. If, in the Piranesi essay, Eisenstein sets in motion a still image, in "Diderot, Brecht, Eisenstein" Barthes freezes the shot, looking for the instantaneity of the tableau. He then writes:

> (Doubtless there would be no difficulty in finding in post-Brechtian theatre and post-Eisensteinian cinema *mises en scène* marked by the dispersion of the tableau, the pulling to pieces of the "composition," the setting in motion of the "partial organs" of the human figure, in short the holding in check of the metaphysical meaning of the work—but then also of its political meaning; or, at least, the carrying over of this meaning towards another politics.)[23]

As the condition of representation in all dioptric arts (theatre, painting, cinema, literature), the tableau realizes the most perfect semiotic enclosure. Everything outside its borders is cast into nonexistence; everything inside is made to share the privileges of light and knowledge—at least insofar as the composition falls under a single point of view and, as Diderot stipulates, its "parts work together to one end and form by their mutual correspondence a unity as real as that of the members of the body of an animal."[24] It is this tableau that will eventually burst out of itself, engendering another shot in the articulation of the montage sequence. "The shot is a montage *cell*," Eisenstein states; as such, it is ready to split and "form a phenomenon of another order, the organism or embryo."[25] Barthes's essay enables us to see that this mutation will occur only after the shot has offered us the "perfect instant," the moment possessing the highest concentration of intelligibility and intensity.[26] What the *"pregnant moment"* holds in balance is not only the story but also the whole of history: past, present, and future, in a simultaneity that does not dismantle teleology but rather anticipates its fulfillment.[27] It is as if the very process of "setting in motion" entailed a secret stillness, a moment of accord before the discharge of the explosion: a guarantee of the totality of both history and the artwork.

Yet the discovery of stillness also holds a potential for deviation. In "The Third Meaning," Barthes again turns Eisenstein's shots into stills, this time shifting his critical attention from the fragment (shot) to the marginal details that the still makes visible. As a result of this process, the narrative does not vanish but loosens its hold on the image, facilitating the development of an "interrogative," "poetical" reading. In a field now open to the free play of signifiers, Barthes finds a meaning that is "evident, erratic, obstinate," a surplus that does not pay off in terms of an economy of fulfilment and discharge.[28] He calls it "obtuse" (blunted, like a rounding that attenuates the impact of the signified) and counts it as "third"—a meaning that is "one 'too many,'" an excess in the very texture of signification. The third meaning is like an internal "fold," a creasing of the image that coincides with a *"slipping away"* of its structuration, a minor and yet persistent disjunction of signifier and signified. That such a slipping away occurs *"from the inside,"* that it coincides with a drifting of meaning (and of desire) in perpetual avoidance of climax: all this suggests that, through Barthes,

Eisenstein's images can engender a transfiguration that is not an explosion. If there is resistance with respect to the totality of the story (and of history), it emerges *within* the image, by virtue of a reading that turns the image itself into a field of potential permutations. Barthes notes that "vertical" reading is not foreign to Eisenstein's own thinking about audiovisual montage and his valorization of the "*inside*" of the shot.[29] However, I will remark, Eisenstein also insists on the necessity of finding the "correct mutual relationship" between shots and their juxtaposition and reiterates that the montage principle ought to promote organic cohesion and consistency, criticizing the absence of perspective characterizing jazz, modern painting, and the American cityscape.[30] On the contrary, Barthes's third meaning is precisely what rejects totalization: "disseminated, reversible, set to its own temporality."[31] It emerges in a suspension of filmic time, as a crease that interrupts montage's all-embracing rhythm. I wonder: what if the eccentricity of the third meaning, its erethism (an excitation too diffuse to be organized under one Law, under one organ), had disturbed Eisenstein's setting in motion of the etching and transformed his viewing of the empty field?

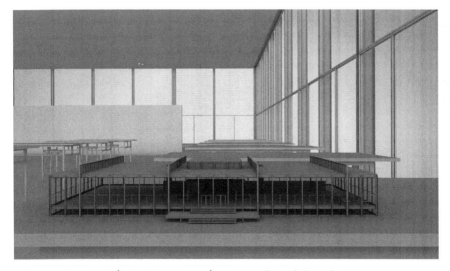

FIGURE 11. *Prairie* (Victor Burgin, 2015): Mies van der Rohe's modernist masterpiece on the Illinois Institute of Technology campus. Courtesy of Victor Burgin.

FIGURE 12. *Prairie* (Victor Burgin, 2015): the dancer leads us through a place in time. Courtesy of Victor Burgin.

FIGURE 13. *Prairie* (Victor Burgin, 2015): the ironwork at the Mecca Flats. Courtesy of Victor Burgin.

PHOTOGRAPHY AS RHYTHM

The intersection of Thirty-Fourth and State lies on the Chicago South Side, in an area that was once known as the "Black Belt."[32] Three stages, ostensibly given to us in reverse chronological order, mark the century-long process of enclosure that has shaped this plot of land. It begins with a photograph we do not see: a short text on black matte describes a group of men and women at the Illinois Institute of Technology in the late 1950s; they are gathered next to metal tables appointed with T-squares; on a table in the foreground lies an architectural model. In another photograph, also briefly described, a dancer poses next to a blackboard filled with architectural calculations; we are told that "her limbs form triangles." What follows is the digital animation of a black-and-white image capturing Crown Hall, Mies van der Rohe's modernist masterpiece at the Illinois Institute of Technology and the alleged setting of both photographs; the hall is empty and we notice a model of the same building on an off-center table. As the camera steadily pulls back toward the foreground, we are brought out of this hall made of steel and glass only to find ourselves in the same space, with the same architectural model, and the camera starting to repeat its backward movement. This time it comes to a halt before leading us out yet again, but the concatenation has quietly established itself and the foreground turned into a depth from which we cannot escape. The modernist masterpiece reproduces itself ad infinitum. In the following images we see the figure of a ballet dancer, ostensibly an African American woman with short curly hair, bending forward, her legs arranged in the shape of a triangle, and then standing, her body turned backward to face walls that hint at a vanished perspectival world. It is as if the stillness of the pose secreted its own duration, in a halt that is not preceded or followed by movement; a suspension of syncopation rather than syncopation as suspension.[33] We are only about to enter the second stage of *Prairie*'s brief history of enclosure and already the interplay of words and images is forming a composition that is difficult to name—an alternation that is almost superimposition, a sequence that defies succession. The impression is that these eccentric tableaux do not follow one another as cinematic shots, perhaps not even as photographs in a series.

The dancer appears to be gently leaning forward, ready to guide us inside and further our memory journey. We learn from a few concise stanzas that the Mecca apartment building occupied this site from 1892 to 1952, when it was razed to make room for the new Illinois Institute of Technology. The text does not rehearse the narrative of urban rise, decline, and renewal through which the Mecca has typically been presented: a luxury building at the turn of the century, an increasingly impoverished and dangerous dwelling after the Depression, a city block reclaimed by the rightful alliance of administrators and architects and put to good use after the war. Instead, it weaves the figures of this lost building through Gwendolyn Brooks's "In the Mecca" (1968), a polyphonic, hybrid poem—an example of resistance through poetic form—in which the author narrates the search for a lost child amid a "labyrinth of stairways, balconies, parlors, and kitchens:"

> Sit where the light corrupts your face.
> Mies van der Rohe retires from grace.
> And the fair fables fall.[34]

We are given no archival pictures of this U-shaped building with multiple entrances, skylit inner courts, and promenade balconies; not during the years when it counted as one of the city's most vital centers of African American culture (the recording of Jimmy Blythe's "Mecca Flats Blues" dates back to 1924), not during the time of its fall into "blight," but we might be familiar with the photos published by *Life* in 1951. What we see is a semicircular camera movement over a surface that resists coming into focus, like the shadow of the floral patterns that adorned the building's wrought-iron staircases and balconies. This is another algorithmic animation, yet now it feels like a gesture of the eyes, almost a caress. The text will soon describe the balconies' "tendrils, leaves, and flowers," the gray terrazzo and the oak-veneered panels, but not before pausing on a photograph captioned "Mecca Tenants Fight—1950," in which composed, well-dressed men and women have gathered in assembly to resist the eviction and, with it, the calculus that has made their lives intolerable for white city officials and urban planners. (I read elsewhere that, upon the completion of Crown Hall, architect Eero Saarinen proclaimed, "Because Chicago is a place of courageous thinking, a slum gives way to a brand new campus—crisp and clean and beautiful and harmonious—a model for a total environment.")[35]

Now the dancer has disappeared and there remains only an empty wall; the light cast on it turns slightly darker, as if the wall were a screen and a projection were about to start. The text that follows is at once spare and luminous, and almost makes visible the intricate surfaces of the Mecca's courts, with their foliated ironwork and precious materials. Then it leads us outside, to the vegetation encircling the building, from Boston ivy to elms and honey locust trees. Here we encounter *Prairie*'s only film image: the low-resolution copy of a black-and-white Western showing covered wagons as they cross the Plains. This dense and orderly caravan is moving toward an off-center point in the background, partitioning the prairie's open space and setting it up as a "place" where the action can occur. Stephen Heath once cogently connected this construction of narrative space with a drive for visual mastery that dates back to Renaissance perspective.[36] But, all in all, the clip looks strangely frail, if only for the sense of precarious materiality it conveys. The last few stanzas offer us a glimpse of what got lost in the controlled depth of this space: the names of the tribes that once inhabited the prairie, the abundance of its wildflowers and the brilliance—and sturdiness—of its grass (the prairie could be wrought only after the invention of the steel blade plow in 1837). The dancer reappears, her arms stretched upward and toward the viewer, her head turned slightly sideways. The foliated panel returns, too, against a black background, the light dancing across its curved lines in an alternation of the gleaming and the opaque. The only depth we see is that of its ornamental surface, which intermittently displays the brilliance of the jewel, or of distant memories. (Is Freud's "dandelion fantasy" that far from this scene of projection?) Despite its intricacy, the panel's arrangement of leaves and flowers maintains a certain symmetry and, with it, an internal hierarchy. But the artificial manipulation of light provokes a confusion, a dispersion of details, a disorder the eye cannot master. Here the *detail*, the indicator of the third meaning, cannot be subsumed by the fragment, the shot in its horizontal and narrative thrust. Instead, it becomes what Naomi Schor has called the "detotalized detail," the mark or blemish of a resistance to the whole that has been historically feminine.[37] The dispersion has taken place. *Prairie* loops back.

Does this dispersion of the tableau, this other setting in motion of the static view, belong to cinema or photography? Or, rather, can we continue to regard the photographic image as essentially still and associate it with instantaneous capture?[38] I will start by noticing that Burgin's *Prairie* reaffirms his career-long interest in the imbrication between space and psychic life. In an interview on conceptual art and photography published in the 1990s, Burgin was already claiming, "It's all about psychical space. That's all my work was ever about." Produced in the last ten years, projection pieces like *Hotel Berlin, A Place to Read, Mirror Lake,* and *Prairie* continue to unfold as theoretical investigations of specific sites: the Tempelhof Airport in Berlin, a former coffeehouse in Istanbul, a Frank Lloyd Wright cottage in Wisconsin, and the intersection of Thirty-Fourth and State in Chicago. These sites exist at the threshold between perception and memory, personal and collective experience, historical erasure and unconscious mnemic persistence. In all cases, Burgin employs the algorithmic animation of still images to express the temporal complexity of the photograph in its very relation to both physical and psychic space, and to explore the "affinity between photography and disappearance," as D. N. Rodowick has suggested.[39] Whether we call them image/text loops or video loops (and we should not underestimate this crisis of naming), they eschew the identical on behalf of "repetition, reprise, recapitulation."[40] For Burgin, it is music and the da capo form rather than cinema that provides us with the best example for understanding these strange loops. He even states, "My videos are uncinematic. I think of my work in video as the pursuit of photography *by other means.*"[41] Indeed, his images challenge not only cinema's construction of space but also the association between duration and cinema as it has developed at the expense of photography, traditionally considered as the medium of instantaneity. "How long is the photograph?" asks Burgin in an article on the last seven minutes of Antonioni's *The Eclipse,* which he experiences as a series of photographs. To the extent that it presents itself as unanswerable, the question prompts us to resist the "reductive *spatialization* of temporality to clock time," typical of capitalistic accumulation, and let the photograph secrete its own time, a duration which it is impossible to quantify.[42]

This question also returns us to the issue of photography's liquid intelligence and the "new displacement of water" that Jeff Wall detects in the transition from analog to electronic and digital media. As water disappears from the production process, "the symbolic meaning of natural forms, made visible in things like turbulence patterns or compound curvatures" constitutes, for Wall, a way to reconnect with photography's archaic past and mobilize dry technics on behalf of transformative memory.[43] In Burgin, the echo of water reverberates at the level not of content per se but of form, in a patterning of the site's duration that remains incalculable not despite but by virtue of digital imaging and the process of passive synthesis it performs. "The panoramic scanning of a still image produces a frame that is 'acompositional' (much as one speaks of the 'atonal' in music)," writes Burgin while discussing the uncinematic qualities of his work. "The contents of the moving frame are in a perpetual state of *de*-composition as the result of the constant, mathematically uniform, passing of all that is visible."[44] It is as if, pushed to its extreme, the dryness of the medium could provide us with the effects of fluidity—an image of becoming or a becoming of the image—that does not require a subject in order to unfold. However, it is my contention that this "*theoretical* vision" constitutes itself not as "incorporeal" or "disembodied" but, rather, as the bearer of a dispersed embodiment, a modulation in which the eye or point of view is but another arrangement of matter. This arrangement—inseparable as it is from its duration—recursively transgresses the conditions of uniformity under which it was produced.[45]

I sit in front of *Prairie* and experience it as one self-differing photograph: a building that opens up into itself, a dancer that endures the injustices of time, wrought-iron leaves fluctuating in the wind of a prairie that was crossed by wagons. This setting in motion of the image in all its components (frame, viewpoint, composition) is not a matter of movement but of rhythm. *Prairie* is this rhythm: a form that does not coalesce, a fluctuating form. Rhythm as rhuthmos resists the reduction of temporality to measurable space; it also, and most importantly, shows that, before any imposition of measure, space and time are profoundly imbricated. To speak of a form that is inseparable from the time of its appearance is to acknowledge the impossibility of isolating the shaping of space from the becoming of time. In "Uncinematic Time," Burgin adopts the term *virtual image* to highlight the constitutive interweaving that, in the psychic economy of the subject, exists between the "real" world of objects and the "imaginary" world of fantasy: what D. W. Winnicott calls "the place where we live" partakes of this dual reality, which remains hard to elucidate as long as we consider space and time as inherently divided.[46] So Burgin turns his attention to Japanese culture and the concept of *ma*: the interval or interstice marking both space and time or, rather, in the words of architect Arata Isozaki: "the moment at which time-and-space had not yet been disentangled and rendered as distinct notions."[47] As Japanese architecture privileges intervals, fissures, and divergences over the fullness of things, so Japanese music pursues "the inner life of the ever-elusive moment" rather than dramatic progression as a succession of moments.[48] Neither punctual nor self-identical, this evanescent moment *(ma)* is deemed inseparable from the movement of becoming *(naru)*. Burgin finds traces of his own "uncinematic" articulation of the visual field in this very interstitial domain. I maintain that the notion of rhuthmos enables us to accomplish another crucial shift of perspective, this time reworking our culture's thinking of forms from the inside. In fact, having been expunged from Western philosophy at an early stage, rhythm as rhuthmos haunts the latter as its constitutive outside, as the reminder of *another* sense of space and time.

Am I proposing that we reconceive of the photographer as a rhythmanalyst? To start with, a rhythmanalyst, writes Henri Lefebvre, is "capable of listening to a house, a street, a town as one listens to a symphony, an opera."[49] For Lefebvre, the world is made up not of inert things but of rhythms—garlands, bundles of rhythms, internal or external, secret or public, or both at the same time, in a crisscrossing of perspectives that positions the rhythmanalyst in more than one place, at more than one time. "To grasp a rhythm," observes Lefebvre, "[it] is necessary to have been *grasped* by it; one must *let oneself go,* give oneself over, abandon oneself to its duration." After Gaston Bachelard's critique of continuity, duration is understood here as fragmentary and heterogeneous rather than unitary and cohesive:

> Overlooking the gardens, the differences between habitual (daily, therefore linked to night and day) rhythms blur; they seem to disappear into a sculptural immobility.... But look harder and longer.... You thus perceive that each plant, each tree, has its rhythm, made up of several: the trees, the flowers, the seeds and fruits, each have their time.[50]

While still holding on to a thought of the instant, in his adoption of rhythm as *method* of analysis Lefebvre resists abstraction and calculation, privileging lived time and what he calls rhythm's internal measure over the external measure of the metronome. To see rhythmically is to see in between simultaneity and succession, to perceive the echo of the image or, as in Burgin's *sequence-image,* to be possessed by a "concatenation that does not take linear form."[51] Such a concatenation, specifies Burgin, "might rather be compared to a rapidly arpeggiated musical chord, the individual notes of which, although sounded successively, vibrate together simultaneously."[52] Neither image nor image sequence, the sequence-image gives us the remembered film as a constellation of elements that can be drawn from diverse spatial and temporal sites, an arrangement that is "fragmentary, circular and repetitive" in the sense adopted by Jean Laplanche and Serge Leclaire to describe fantasies and daydreams.[53] In the case of digital projections, it is as if the gallery functioned as a luminous darkroom, the site of a development or flashing up of the image that is akin to what happens in the psychoanalytic session. Projection names here the workings of both light and the unconscious, in a paradoxical coiling or folding of the geometric line that releases the subject from the constraints of the perspectival system.

In *How to Live Together,* Barthes starts exploring the intimate relationship between rhythm and power by foregrounding a minor episode:

> From my window (December 1, 1976), I see a mother pushing an empty stroller, holding her child by the hand. She walks at her own pace, imperturbably; the child, meanwhile, is being pulled, dragged along, is forced to keep running, like an animal, or one of Sade's victims being whipped. She walks at her own pace, unaware of the fact that her son's rhythm is different. And she's his mother![54]

Against the grain of this scene, he returns to the marginalized notion of rhuthmos to explore the fantasy of a Living-Together that is "neither dual nor collective" but, rather, something that realizes "the paradox, the contradiction, the aporia of bringing distances together—the utopia of a socialism of distances." As a "subtle form" that also includes mood swings (the alternation of depression and elation, for instance), *idiorrhythmy* is "the exact opposite of an inflexible, implacably regular cadence";[55] it requires a distance from the world, a withdrawal punctuated by interruptions that are not regulated by any strong formation of power (large communes, phalansteries, convents, etc.), like in the case of Mount Athos's monastic clusters; it articulates a field of diffuse desire. Following Benveniste's interpretation, the term *rhuthmos* would suffice to suggest such a fluctuation: if it becomes necessary to attach the prefix *idio-* (distinct, peculiar), it is because power has repeatedly appropriated *rhythm,* its definition and its manifestations. "Before anything else," writes Barthes, "the first thing that power imposes is a rhythm (to everything: a rhythm of life, of time, of thought, of speech). The demand of idiorrhythmy is always made in opposition to power." At this juncture, music is explicitly equated to power and found to be antithetical to rhuthmos. What Barthes is after is "a rhythm that allows for approximation, for imperfection, for a supplement, a lack, and *idios*: what doesn't fit the structure, or would have to be made to fit."[56] We could detect in this last remark an implicit reference to *biopower*, which Michel Foucault had begun to discuss in his lecture course at the Collège de France only the previous year (1975–76): "power's hold over life," "the power to 'make' live and 'let' die," in which racism plays a key productive role.[57] Apropos of Foucault, Deleuze will write that "life becomes resistance to power when power takes life as its object."[58] It is in this context that rhuthmos becomes a form of resistance, indeed resistance as form—as the form that life takes in opposition to power.[59] With rhuthmos, we find the configuring of a "subject *(idios)*"[60] that is singular, that is not "made to fit": neither an individual nor the member of an organized collective, this subject emerges only in or, rather, *as* an idiorrhythmic cluster.

What I consider invaluable is that Barthes connects this power "over life" not only to the imposition of a structured (musical) rhythm but also to the production of fixed visual forms. He reminds us that, within the history of Western culture, the rectangle, of which the pictorial frame is an adaptation, constitutes "the basic shape of power": the *Rex* is "someone who draws straight lines," and the *Regula* is both the authoritative rule for communal life and "the instrument used to draw a straight line." It is in the context of idiorrhythmy that Barthes discusses the enclosure's double function of protection and definition. If the former entails the "transformation of territory into property," the latter coincides with the very drawing of lines: "to define" is "to mark out borders, frontiers." The rectangle and the frame partake of this history of the enclosure, which is also a history of the straight line, while rhythm as rhuthmos operates against them. A singular and impermanent form "but a form nonetheless," this other rhythm works in opposition to any authoritative demarcation, any rigid partitioning of space and time, opening up both to dispersion, disorder, decomposition. The pictorial or photographic frame, too, needs to be caught in this process of destabilization. Again, Barthes's interest in the "function of the round (of the rounded)"—and what is the third meaning, if not obtuse, blunted?—arises in relation to questions of subversion. In their circular form, the tent and the theater of antiquity offer the most overtly defiant model, but Western art since Paul Cézanne, Oriental painting, and comic strips have also partaken in this attempt to fight "the tyranny of regulatory lines" that has long partitioned the space we inhabit. However, Barthes points out, "the subversion of a shape, of an archetype is not necessarily effected by its opposite but by more subtle means, by retaining the shape and inventing a distinctive play of superimposition for it, or one of effacement, of overstepping its limits."[61] This is what *Prairie* performs for its viewers: an undoing of forms that challenges the very way in which we conceive of them. To say that *Prairie* is a place of rhythm is thus also to foreground the piece's complex reworking of "the pictorial space inaugurated by the invention of perspective," a mode of image-making that, for Burgin, comprises both photography and 3D computer modeling.[62] If the straight line is essential to the calculus of the perspectival system, *Prairie* offers us the example of a practice of photography that makes this line provisional, curved or coiled—like in the Mecca's lost ironwork—too evanescent to hold.

At once tentative and recursive, rhythm as rhuthmos operates against the homogeneous ordering not only of space but also of time; it discloses time's depth against the tyranny of the instant and of chronology as a succession of instants, or points in time, generating a heterogeneity that cannot be subsumed under one measure. It is at this juncture that my interpretation of *Prairie*, as a place of rhythm, interlocks with my claim that such a place belongs to the field of photography. In other words: *Prairie* points to, traces, and indeed *photographs* an overlay in the history of the same site, to the very extent that it comprises not a fixed view, but a constellation of fleeting images. By radically intervening in the cohesion of frame, composition, and point of view, *Prairie* makes visible this temporal layering, beyond the opposition of simultaneity and succession; it registers it as "intermittence"—as "the staging of an appearance-as-disappearance," to borrow Barthes's striking formulation.[63] How, then, can Burgin's piece, and the rhythm it performs, help us rethink medium specificity and photography's indexical properties? What does it mean to practice photography *by other means,* if we shift our critical attention to rhythm and the disturbance of mediatic properties that it entails? In particular, what needs to be tested yet again is the obsession with the instant and the instantaneous, and the role it has played in defining photography as the medium capable of, and, indeed, entitled to "testify to a *present* state of affairs"—to capture that which allegedly takes place once, and only once, at a precise point in time, in front of the camera lens.[64]

In his contribution to the collection *Projective: Essays about the Work of Victor Burgin*, Rodowick states that Burgin's new gallery works constitute the virtual materialization of sequence-images and that, as such, they mark the "disappearance of photography in the digital image."[65] While concurring on their innovative force, I will nevertheless propose that we consider these works—*Prairie* in particular—as constitutive examples of photography's "expanding field." I borrow the term from Peter Osborne, who theorizes the unity of the photographic as distributive—an aesthetic and pragmatic unity in which heterogeneous and continuously evolving image technologies are held together by common cultural functions. What digital imaging threatens is an "imagined unity," an originary coherence predicated on the identification of "a particular technological process (optical/mechanical/chemical) and a particular set of social functions (the solemnization of festivity / documentation / pornography / advertising / surveillance, etc.)." Osborne underscores how this reduction of the photographic to the still photograph hinges on "the idea of the 'capture' of a moment in time," on the fiction of the instant.[66] If there is no instant to be grasped or missed, it becomes impossible to answer not only the question, "Where is the photograph?" (as Osborne suggests) but also its more intangible counterpart, "When is the photograph?"—when does it take place, how long does it last? I believe that Burgin's work enables us to push even further this operation of dispossession with respect to photography's phantasmatic unity and think the photographic image as a rhythmic, self-differing configuration. Let me state it more directly: *Prairie* points us toward the *reinvention* of photography as rhythm.[67] In its folding–unfolding of views of the same site, it traces the contours of a *here* that keeps disappearing as *now*, emerging instead as a complex modulation of the sensible—a rhythm or pattern made of dancers, leaves, flowers, and words describing other invisible photographs. Unlike the narrative film sequence, this constellation appears as a superimposition that unfolds while also withdrawing.

"LIVING AT THE SAME TIME AS . . ."

Why am I so committed to finding rhuthmos, and the irregularly differentiated duration it entails, at the heart of Burgin's new photographic practice? In *Prairie,* the brief shot of wagons follows a spare, careful description of the Mecca's atrium and the surrounding park as they were before the demolition. It is followed by the words: "Settlers crossing Illinois in Spring at the time of the Indian Wars marveled at the brilliant grassland and swells of abundant wildflowers / They could not plow the prairie until 1837 when a blacksmith invented the steel blade plow / They said the sound of tearing roots was like the rattling fire of infantry in battle." Photography as rhythm portrays this history of enclosure, which is also a history of violence, while maintaining the greatest distance from the logic of instrumentality that Allan Sekula finds at work throughout the history of photography. In his analysis of Edward Steichen's activity during World War I, Sekula remarks precisely on the temporality of military vision, with its dream of instantaneity: "The value of aerial photographs, as cues for military action, depended on their ability to testify to a *present* state of affairs."[68] Or, in the words of a former U.S. secretary of defense, quoted by Paul Virilio in *War and Cinema,* "Once you can see the target, you can expect to destroy it."[69] Photography and war meet most keenly at this juncture—when time itself becomes a target. By unfurling in time rather than standing, holding its ground in some fictional now-point, *Prairie* subverts this goal-oriented logic and its demand for instantaneity. Indeed, as an ephemeral and yet recurring form, it shows us that, to borrow Maurice Merleau-Ponty's words, "even in the present, the landscape is a configuration," that the landscape around us does not relate to other times in an external and sequential manner but holds them inside or behind itself, *almost* simultaneously, in a play of visibility and invisibility.[70] (I say "almost" to underscore that this simultaneity is not a matter of "all at once" or of a retroactively attained cohesion: the piece unfolds through indefinite sliding rather than encasement, displacement rather than substitution.)[71] It is among the tasks of photography to register this paradoxical persistence—the endurance of fleeting configurations—against the imposition of temporal boundaries and the writing of official history.

At the beginning of his lecture course, Barthes remarks that Living-Together always occurs in time. While fundamentally involving space, the fantasy of idiorrhythmy also unfolds in the dimension of "contemporaneity":

> As a fantastical digression, this: it goes without saying that we'll be thinking of Living-Together as an essentially spatial fact (living together in the same space). But in its most basic form Living-Together is also temporal.... "living at the same time as..." "living in the same time as..."[72]

Barthes does not further explore the questions "Who are my contemporaries? Whom do I live with?" but notices that calendar time will not offer much guidance in this respect, leaving open the possibility of a concomitance that transpires across time or, rather, in a time that is an overlay of past and present. Indeed, Barthes's own gathering of literary texts and historical records suggests that a lifestyle also takes shape by virtue of semiotic encounters of all kinds. By privileging culture or non-method, Barthes turns his own lecture course into a place of anachronistic and creative misalliances.[73] I now think of Burgin's *Prairie* as a version of this particular fantasy—inhabiting the same space in a heterogeneous, internally differentiated time. Photography as rhythm actualizes a Living-Together that takes shape in the coils of time, through the undoing of temporal borders. In Eisenstein's Piranesi essay, the field that was once an apple orchard ultimately remains empty, the present connecting to the past in an external or sequential manner rather than becoming contemporaneous with it. On the other hand, *Prairie* reworks the relationship between proximity and distance, appearance and disappearance from *within,* displaying something other than a linkage between shots. Here idiorrhythmy brings together not only subjects (the viewer, the photographer, the people of the Mecca and of the prairie) but also images—those images of the world emerging in between perception and memory through which our subjectivity is constituted. Indeed, by arranging them in a carefully unresolved manner, this idiosyncratic photograph lets us glimpse other ways in which "subjects" can come into being and live together in a relationship of intimate distance. It prompts us to reconfigure and counter the still-enduring violence that has shaped our cities while forging what Naoki Sakai calls a "nonaggregate community," one in which "we are together and can address ourselves as 'we' because we are distant from one another and because our togetherness is not grounded on any common homogeneity."[74] For Sakai, this reinvention of sociality passes through a process of translation that refuses to mobilize the "'we' of national affiliation or the 'we' of cultural or civilizational commonality," recognizing instead the irreducible heterogeneity that sustains and expands our "being-in-common."[75] The distinction between "homolingual" and "heterolingual" address pivots around the recourse to a uniform measure of value: if the former obeys a logic of equivalence, producing identities out of differences, the latter enables hybrid "fragments" of cultural discourse to come together in "new and accidental ways," in precarious arrangements, if you will. The subject of this other mode of translation is not the "epistemic subject *(shukan),*" which "emerges in the spatiality of synchronicity," but the "practical agent *(shutai),*" which "always flees such spatiality and can never be present to itself either," inhabiting instead time as differentiated duration.[76]

THE OPEN INSTANT

In her essay "The Im/Pulse to See," Rosalind Krauss takes issue with the dream of instantaneity, as it relates to modernist painting's pursuit of "an abstracted and heightened visuality":

> "Do you know who Frank [Stella] thinks is the greatest living American?" Michael [Fried] asked me one day. And then, grinning at the sheer brilliance of the answer, he said it was Ted Williams, the great hitter of the Red Sox. "He sees faster than any living human," Michael said. "His vision is so fast that he can see the stitching on the baseball as it comes over the plate. Ninety miles an hour, but he sees the stitches. So he hits the ball out of the park. That's why Frank thinks he's a genius."[77]

The autonomy of vision heralded by critics such as Clement Greenberg and Michael Fried relied on, indeed *demanded,* a particular demarcation, not only of space, but also of time. What I have called temporal enclosure reaches here its own peculiar apex, at least outside the domain of photography. Krauss's anecdote exposes a chain of imaginary male identifications: the player, cherished by the artist, cherished by the critic, is someone who allegedly sees outside of duration, in a moment of pure presentness. To this model of enhanced, almost immaterial vision, Krauss counterposes the workings of "a rhythm, or beat, or pulse—a kind of throb of on/off on/off on/off" that destabilizes vision with respect to both space and time.[78] What I find invaluable in Krauss's account is her emphasis on two interlaced aspects of this other visuality. First, she understands the disturbance produced by the anti-modernist beat in terms of *form*: space and time lose clarity and immediacy as form is acted against, repeatedly submitted to a process of dissolution. Second, such a re-working, indeed un-working of form characterizes vision through and through; it is not an accidental mutation but, rather, an internal, constitutive transgression.

Following Jean-François Lyotard's research on the figural, Krauss adopts the term *matrix* to name this domain in excess of structure, an order that is invisible, unconscious and irreducible to external space. The matrix is a form, and yet, a form that can only undo itself, over and over, in the activity of a beat or pulse whose regularity ensnares the subject's unconscious. "On/off on/off on/off" is the rhythm marking the charge and discharge of pleasure, the time signature of fantasies, dreams, and symptoms, as exemplified by Freud's account of "A Child Is Being Beaten."[79] Ernst's bird flights, Duchamp's spirals, Giacometti's oscillating ball emerge as recurring patterns—as patterns of recurrence—out of this matrix, reenacting, performing anew the very throb of desire that has propelled their formation. This irruption of temporality greatly upsets the modernist dream, making it impossible to preserve a "distinctness" of domains.[80] However, it does not suffice to dismantle it. In fact, Krauss's adoption of an on/off model reduces rhythm to a cadence, bolstering rather than undermining its subordination to measure, in a way that recalls her treatment of compulsion discussed in the second chapter. It is measure—the measurement of time and its concomitant subordination to motion—that grounded the thought of instantaneity, which Krauss is now taking to task.[81] In the throb, measure returns in a disguised fashion, producing a doubling of the instant that, while affecting the coherence of the subject, still binds its desire to the law of numbers. No longer in charge of counting, the subject becomes the one who is counted—or, rather, caught up in a system that counts. If the eroticism that Krauss uncovers in her examples might be said to conform to this model, the question of another modulation of desire continues to persist.

Another artist, a modernist filmmaker according to most accounts—this time, however, not hitting the target, the bull's eye, but missing it in an elusive manner. The last seven minutes of Antonioni's *The Eclipse* represent one of the most celebrated sequences in film history—an arrangement of fifty-seven shots describing a peripheral city corner and its immediate surroundings, registering the life of people and things during a period of uncertain duration (it begins sometime in the afternoon and ends in the early evening). In the previous sequence, which takes place at around midday in the center of Rome, Piero (Alain Delon) and Vittoria (Monica Vitti) agree to see each other again that evening. Piero, a stockbroker, who clearly understands that time is money, is quite specific about the rendezvous: "At eight o'clock. Same place." The place in question is a nondescriptive corner in the modern EUR district, where Vittoria lives by herself, working as a translator.[82] Among the few distinguishable markers are a house under construction, a wooden fence, a pile of bricks, and a barrel of water. During a previous meeting, Vittoria finds a piece of wood in the water and gently plays with it; later, Piero tosses an empty book of matches into the same barrel. The barrel and the discarded objects reappear more than once in the final sequence, but this time no one is standing next to them. In fact, we will never even catch sight of the protagonists again. We will never know whether their love story has come to an end, or whether they missed each other only on that occasion, or whether it is Antonioni's camera that missed the appointment. Here, I propose that we regard this sequence as an experiment on how one can miss the decisive moment and, instead, register the surface of the world as an irregular rhythmic patterning. The subject of this vision remains impersonal and dispersed throughout the very surface that is supposed to constitute its counterpart. Yet, it is important to notice that it finds its precursor in Vittoria's floating perception, an openness to encounter and linger with the world's images and sounds that she shares with the other female protagonists in Antonioni's tetralogy.[83]

What we perceive is hard to recall in exact order, as the sequence deftly blurs the distinction between simultaneity and succession: wide and medium shots of quasi-deserted streets, close-ups of leaves, ants, tree trunks, muddy soil, leaking barrels, automatic sprinklers, drops of water, the grass, the asphalt, crosswalks, utility holes. The few people are either standing, waiting for nothing in particular, or walking; some we have noticed before (a harness horse racer, a nanny in uniform), others we almost mistake for

FIGURE 14. *L'Eclisse* (Michelangelo Antonioni, 1962): Vitti and Delon's missed appointment or, "at eight o'clock, same place."

the protagonists. As seen by Antonioni's camera, the surface of the world is an overlay of smaller and larger fluctuations. A sense of stillness pervades the sequence and yet this stillness cannot be equated with immobility—where nothing occurs, we are left with the quivering of things, their internal vibrations. Natural sounds and noises, too, yield their own punctuation: the wind, the rustling leaves, water gushing out of a barrel, the clip-clop of a horse, a bus jump-starting its engine, another one steering abruptly, a faraway jet plane, and footsteps. At once concrete and spare, they contribute to creating a sense of haunted tranquility, like the slowing down of a heartbeat. We almost do not need to read about the atomic bomb on the front page of a newspaper held by a passerby; but when we do, anxiety congeals only for a few moments. This is not Alfred Hitchcock's "Four O'Clock" TV episode, where the protagonist is accidentally tied up next to the bomb he set up to explode and the spectator trembles with him.[84] Nor is it Chris Marker's *La Jetée* (1962), even if the latter might be easily summoned up by shots of a man on a rooftop pointing toward the sky, a jet trail over the horizon line, and a stark light tower. There is no pregnant moment, no ecstatic violence—only a muted, pervasive disorientation, a malaise in which we almost feel at home.

It is true that, as Seymour Chatman has observed, the final sequence could be considered "an establishing shot in reverse,"[85] as here we are finally given that overview of the EUR district withheld at the beginning. But this is a false establishing shot: rather than gaining retrospective clarity, we soon lose any capacity to keep track, to orient ourselves in space and time. To the photograph, for which the words "eight o'clock, same place" would constitute an apt caption, Antonioni substitutes a coda that expands, de-contracts, opens up the enclosure of the instant. Yet this is not the explosion but the unfettering of the now-point, its mutation into a time of indefinite duration, with no center and no subject. One could speak of a "time of the world," but only at the risk of eliciting a connection with the Aristotelian tradition of measuring time that the film leaves behind.[86] In fact, the coda constitutes the overturning of the minute of silence that, early in the film, is held at the Rome Stock Exchange to commemorate the death of a broker. The scene also marks the couple's first encounter. "A minute, here, is worth millions," Piero murmurs to Vittoria, inadvertently exposing his own character and, more important, the system that has produced it. If a "minute" would become an obsolete measuring unit in the age of global finance capitalism, which for Virilio coincides with a new economy of speed, the emphasis on the value of time outside the sphere of production proper maintains its urgency.[87] In the coda, the clock time of capital is not forgotten but left aside, or behind, as if people and things could temporarily live together in the fantasy of a delayed, uncanny duration.[88] Unlike the minute of silence at the stock exchange, this duration emerges as a configuration that is at once carefully woven and imperfect, precarious, held together by creases and lines of flight. There is no on/off pattern structuring the visual montage, no beat governing our desire. The atonal music and the layering of notes, too, contribute to a sense of horizontal, non-teleological dilation. We gradually get used to this want of dramatic progression and give in to our incapacity to predict what comes next. The false diegetic clues interspersing the shots, promissory notes for a scenario that never materializes, begin to subsist as traces of a narrative universe that has retreated, or is yet to return. Indeed the last shot, with its overblown light and the same musical fragment that had accompanied the title sequence, signals that the film is ready to loop back, that perhaps this night will lead back to the dawn that had opened it.

Reworking, reinventing a medium as "a set of conventions derived from (but not identical with) the material conditions of a given technical support" also entails revising the conditions of intelligibility that have propelled its development.[89] In the case of photography and cinema, the drive to capture the instant has provided both the springboard and the objective for elaborating an aesthetics that has often kept vision's transformative potential in check. Rhythm as eccentric configuration works against the instant as temporal enclosure, one that our new economy has only made more minute and thus more difficult to detect. In Burgin's *Prairie,* such a rhythmic dilation of the instant unfolds as a journey into the depth of time, dismantling the ostensive self-presence of place and the erasures that such a fiction entails. In Antonioni's *The Eclipse,* the instant expands in a coexistence that is not atemporal but, rather, inhabits the horizontal time of a differentiated and yet unmeasurable duration. In both cases, instantaneity dissolves into simultaneity as difference, while the strangely compact, overlaid temporality of fantasy envelops and transforms the chronology of objective reality. Having become external and impersonal, fantasy permeates vision through and through, tracing and pointing toward other ways of inhabiting the world. Like in Barthes's stills, here we perceive not independently of the diegetic horizon but, rather, against or beyond it. What we see is simultaneity as the difference we have in common.

Notes

INTRODUCTION

1. See Miriam Bratu Hansen, "Room for Play: Benjamin's Gamble with Cinema," *October* 109 (Summer 2004): 3–45.

2. Donna Haraway, "A Manifesto for Cyborgs: Science, Technology, and Socialist Feminism in the 1980s," *Socialist Review* 80 (1985): 65–108.

3. Jean-François Lyotard, "Acinema," in *Narrative, Apparatus, Ideology*, ed. Philip Rosen (New York: Columbia University Press, 1986), 350–51.

4. Jean-Joseph Goux, *Symbolic Economies: After Marx and Freud*, trans. Jennifer Curtiss Gage (Ithaca, N.Y.: Cornell University Press, 1990). Goux explains how the general equivalent enjoys an utterly privileged status: "a hierarchy is instituted between an excluded, idealized element and the other elements, which measure their value in it" (4). Its logic extends to culture at large as "the *Father* becomes the general equivalent of subjects, *Language* the general equivalent of signs, and the *Phallus* the general equivalent of objects, in a way that is structurally and genetically homologous to the accession of a unique element (let us say *Gold*, for the sake of simplicity) to the rank of the general equivalent of products" (4).

5. Lyotard, "Acinema," 352.

6. Lyotard, 353.

7. On Lyotard's changing view of narrative cinema, especially Italian Neorealism, see Ashley Woodward, "A Sacrificial Economy of the Image: Lyotard on Cinema," *Angelaki* 19, no. 4 (2014): 141–54.

8. Jean-François Lyotard, "The Unconscious as Mise-en-scène," in *Performance in Postmodern Culture*, ed. Michel Benamou and Charles Caramello (Madison, Wis.: Coda Press, 1977), 98.

9. Antonio Negri, "Art and Culture in the Age of Empire and the Time of the Multitudes," *SubStance* 36, no. 1 (2007): 52. For the distinction between "outside measure" and "beyond measure," see Michael Hardt and Antonio Negri, *Empire* (Cambridge, Mass.: Harvard University Press, 2000).

10. Andrea Righi, "Origin and Dismeasure: The Thought of Sexual Difference in Luisa Muraro and Ida Dominijanni, and the Rise of Post-Fordist Psychopathology," in *Another Mother: Diotima and the Symbolic Order of Italian Feminism*, ed. Cesare Casarino and Andrea Righi, trans. Mark William Epstein (Minneapolis: University of Minnesota Press, 2018), 265.

11. Émile Benveniste, "The Notion of Rhythm in Its Linguistic Expression," in *Problems in General Linguistics*, trans. Mary Elizabeth Meek (Coral Gables, FL: University of Miami Press, 1971), 285–86.

12. Henri Meschonnic, *Critique du rythme: Anthropologie historique du langage* (Paris: Verdier, 2009).

13. Gilles Deleuze and Félix Guattari, *A Thousand Plateaus: Capitalism and Schizophrenia*, trans. Brian Massumi (Minneapolis: University of Minnesota Press, 1987), 363.

14. Benveniste, "Notion of Rhythm," 287.

15. See Gilles Deleuze, "Immanence: A Life," in *Pure Immanence: Essays on A Life*, trans. Anne Boyman (Cambridge, Mass.: MIT Press, 2001).

16. Souleymane Bachir Diagne, *African Art as Philosophy: Senghor, Bergson and the Idea of Negritude* (Kolkata: Seagull Books, 2012); Jessica Wiskus, *The Rhythm of Thought: Art, Literature, and Music after Merleau-Ponty* (Chicago: University of Chicago Press, 2013).

17. Diagne, 101.

18. Léopold Sédar Senghor, "What the Black Man Contributes," in *Race and Racism in Continental Philosophy*, ed. Robert Bernasconi (Bloomington: Indiana University Press, 2003), 296.

19. Senghor; see also Diagne, *African Art as Philosophy*, 79.

20. Maurice Merleau-Ponty, *Notes des cours au Collège de France, 1958–1959 et 1960–1961*, ed. Stéphanie Ménasé (Paris: Éditions Gallimard, 1996), 199, cit. and trans. in Wiskus, *Rhythm of Thought*, 111.

21. Maurice Merleau-Ponty, "Working Notes," in *The Visible and the Invisible*, ed. Claude Lefort, trans. Alphonso Lingis (Evanston, Ill.: Northwestern University Press, 1968), 225.

22. Ewa Plonowska Ziarek, *Feminist Aesthetics and the Politics of Modernism* (New York: Columbia University Press, 2012), 124.

23. Caroline Levine, *Forms: Whole, Rhythm, Hierarchy, Network* (Princeton, N.J.: Princeton University Press, 2015), 3.

24. Deleuze writes that "life becomes resistance to power when power takes life as its object." In Gilles Deleuze, *Foucault*, trans. Sean Hand (Minneapolis: University of Minnesota, 1995), 92.

1. LIFE

1. Kaja Silverman, *The Threshold of the Visible World* (New York: Routledge, 1996); Nora M. Alter, "The Political Im/perceptible in the Essay Film: Farocki's 'Images of the World and the Inscription of War,'" *New German Critique* 68 (1996): 165–92; Thomas Keenan, "Light Weapons," *Documents* 1–2 (1992): 147–58.

2. See, for instance, Alter, "Political Im/perceptible"; and Silverman, *Threshold of the Visible World*.

3. Silverman, *Threshold of the Visible World*, 138.

4. Silverman, 143; more specifically, Silverman claims that, in a turn or twist of resistance, *Bilder* mobilizes the porosity and flexibility of the look against the rigidity and imperviousness of the camera/gaze, that is, against the very apparatus that is responsible for its own production.

5. See Marjorie Haas, "Fluid Thinking: Irigaray's Critique of Formal Logic," in *Representing Reason: Feminist Theory and Formal Logic*, ed. Rachel Joffe Falmagne and Marjorie Haas (Lanham, Md.: Rowman & Littlefield, 2002), 71–88. For an alternative critique, see *A Thousand Plateaus*, where Deleuze and Guattari appeal to Michel Serres's return to ancient atomism and the geometry of Archimedes to find a hydraulic model that does not treat fluids as a special case of a theory of solids, "a model of becoming and heterogeneity," an example of minor or nomadic science. Gilles Deleuze and Félix Guattari, *A Thousand Plateaus: Capitalism and Schizophrenia*, trans. Brian Massumi (Minneapolis: University of Minnesota Press, 1987), 361, 489.

6. Luce Irigaray, "The 'Mechanics' of Fluids," in *This Sex Which Is Not One*, trans. Catherine Porter and Carolyn Burke (Ithaca, N.Y.: Cornell University Press, 1985), 107.

7. Luce Irigaray, "Volume without Contours," in *The Irigaray Reader*, ed. Margaret Whitford (Cambridge, Mass.: Basil Blackwell, 1991), 64; Irigaray, "'Mechanics' of Fluids," 110 (emphasis in original).

8. Irigaray, "Volume without Contours," 66; Irigaray, "'Mechanics' of Fluids," 112. "Woman" appears as "(the/a) woman" in the former and "awoman" in the latter. For a discussion on metaphor and metonymy, see the next chapter.

9. Irigaray, "'Mechanics' of Fluids," 114 (emphasis in original).

10. Irigaray, "Volume without Contours," 64.

11. N. Katherine Hayles, "Gender Encoding in Fluid Mechanics: Masculine Channels and Feminine Flows," *differences* 4 (Summer 1992): 19. For instance,

Hayles writes, "In the same way that women are erased within masculinist theories and languages, existing only as not-men, so fluids have been erased from science, existing only as non-solids" (17).

12. Luce Irigaray, "The Power of Discourse and the Subordination of the Feminine," in *This Sex Which Is Not One*, trans. Catherine Porter and Carolyn Burke (Ithaca, N.Y.: Cornell University Press, 1985), 72.

13. Ewa Plonowska Ziarek, "Toward a Radical Female Imaginary: Temporality and Embodiment in Irigaray's Ethics," *Diacritics* 28, no. 1 (1998): 67.

14. Irigaray, "'Mechanics' of Fluids," 112; see also Plonowska Ziarek, "Toward a Radical Female Imaginary," 62, on attributing to the mirror image a paradoxical but "essential resistance to the elusive process of Becoming."

15. Plonowska Ziarek, "Toward a Radical Female Imaginary," 67.

16. Irigaray, "Volume without Contours," 55.

17. Jeff Wall, "Photography and Liquid Intelligence," in *Jeff Wall: Selected Essays and Interviews*, ed. Peter Galassi (New York: Museum of Modern Art, 2007), 109–10.

18. Wall, 109. He adds, "Water—symbolically—represents an 'archaism' in photography, one that is admitted into the process, but also excluded, contained, or channeled by its hydraulics."

19. In *Threshold of the Visible World*, Silverman writes of the look's capacity "to reanimate and open to change" (160) even the very images that were initially mass-produced.

20. In quotation marks are excerpts from *Bilder*'s voice-over text. Kaja Silverman might have been inspired by the film when she writes about Wall's essay in *The Miracle of Analogy* (Stanford, Calif.: Stanford University Press, 2015). Here she seems to resolve the opposition between photography and hand drawing, camera/gaze and look, by reconceiving of photography as analogy, revelation rather than inscription, a summoning to see the "authorless and untranscendable similarities that structure Being, or . . . 'the world,' and that give everything the same ontological weight" (11). However, by underscoring that "every analogy contains both similarity and difference" and distinguishing between "amount[s] of difference," Silverman treats difference as secondary and measurable; not surprisingly, she suggests that it constitutes what needs to be bridged in order "to maintain the 'two-in-one' principle" according to which analogy works (11–12).

21. Wall, "Photography and Liquid Intelligence," 109.

22. Wall, 109.

23. "*Whatever can see wants to be seen,*" writes Arendt, "*whatever can hear calls out to be heard, whatever can touch presents itself to be touched.*" Hannah Arendt, *The Life of the Mind* (New York: Harcourt Brace Jovanovich, 1978), 29 (emphasis

Notes to Chapter 1

in original). See Kaja Silverman, *World Spectators* (Stanford, Calif.: Stanford University Press, 2000) for a theory of perceptual signification that builds on it, and my own "The Actress as Filmmaker: On Ingrid Bergman and Roberto Rossellini's New Erotics of Vision," *World Picture* 7 (2012): http://www.worldpicturejournal-com/WP_7/Torlasco.html, for a phenomenological interpretation of the relationship between passivity and activity.

24. Wall, "Photography and Liquid Intelligence," 110.

25. Gaston Bachelard, *Water and Dreams: An Essay on the Imagination of Matter*, 3rd ed., trans. Edith R. Farrell (Dallas: Dallas Institute of Humanities and Culture, 1999).

26. Émile Benveniste, "The Notion of 'Rhythm' in Its Linguistic Expression," in *Problems in General Linguistics*, trans. Mary Elizabeth Meek (Coral Gables, Fla.: University of Miami Press, 1971), 285–86.

27. For another treatment of "liquid perception" see Gilles Deleuze, *Cinema 1: The Movement-Image*, trans. Hugh Tomlinson and Barbara Habberjam (Minneapolis: University of Minnesota Press, 2001).

28. Benveniste, "Notion of 'Rhythm,'" 280–88.

29. Citations from Archilochus and Aeschylus seem to confirm that, in these cases at least, rhythm is what holds or bounds, thus imposing itself as a form that possesses consistency and permanence. The most notable criticism comes from Serres, who in *The Birth of Physics* reproaches Benveniste for starting from language rather than reality and therefore missing the vortexes of the fluvial streams. Michel Serres, *The Birth of Physics*, trans. Jack Hawkes (Manchester, UK: Clinamen, 2001).

30. Deleuze and Guattari, *Thousand Plateaus*, 363. In their support of Serres's *The Birth of Physics*, they rephrase Benveniste's rhuthmos as the "form of a 'measured, cadenced' movement." While supportive of Benveniste, Gasché treats *rhuthmos* as if it were interchangeable with *schema*. See Rodolphe Gasché, *Of Minimal Things: Studies on the Notion of Relation* (Stanford, Calif.: Stanford University Press, 1999).

31. Benveniste, "Notion of 'Rhythm,'" 283.

32. This passage is cited in Benveniste, 284.

33. Benveniste, 285–86.

34. Philippe Lacoue-Labarthe, "The Echo of the Subject," in *Typography: Mimesis, Philosophy, Politics*, by Philippe Lacoue-Labarthe, ed. Christopher Fynsk (Stanford, Calif.: Stanford University Press, 1998), 201.

35. Philippe Lacoue-Labarthe, "Caesura of the Speculative," in *Typography: Mimesis, Philosophy, Politics*, by Philippe Lacoue-Labarthe, ed. Christopher Fynsk (Stanford, Calif.: Stanford University Press, 1998), 221. Apropos of this most

elusive flux, it might be helpful to remember an anecdote in which a disciple of Heraclitus, Kratylos, "criticized Heraclitus for saying that one cannot enter the same river twice, for he himself held that it cannot be done even once." Aristotle, *Metaphysics, Volume I: Books 1–9,* trans. Hugh Tredennick (Cambridge, Mass.: Harvard University Press, 1933), 189. See also Søren Kierkegaard, *Fear and Trembling,* trans. Sylvia Walsh (Cambridge, UK: Cambridge University Press, 2006), 109. My thanks to Sam Weber for directing my attention toward this passage.

36. Plato, *Laws* 665a, cit. in Benveniste, "Notion of 'Rhythm,'" 287.

37. Benveniste, 287.

38. See Pierre Sauvanet, *Le Rythme grec: d'Héraclite à Aristote* (Paris: Presses universitaires de France, 1999), 85.

39. Sauvanet, 84; however, it is Aristotle who renders *rhuthmos* with *skhema* in the *Metaphysics* and "schematizes" *rhuthmos* in the *Poetics*: "In dancing, rhythm [*rhuthmos*] alone is used without 'harmony'; for even dancing imitates character, emotion, and action, by rhythmical movement [*schematizomenoi rhuthmoi*]." Aristotle, *The Poetics of Aristotle,* trans. S. H. Butcher (London: Macmillan, 1902), 9.

40. Lacoue-Labarthe, "Echo of the Subject," 202.

41. Lacoue-Labarthe, 202. Elsewhere, *rhuthmizein* comes to mean "to give form" as in "to discipline"; see Sauvanet, *Le Rythme grec,* 82.

42. It should be remembered that Greek *mousike* comprised both musical and verbal components; see Sauvanet, *Le Rythme grec.* When Derrida succinctly points out the political valence of Lacoue-Labarthe's essay on resonance and the proliferation of specular images, he has in mind the dangers of a politics of identification pursued through mimesis. Jacques Derrida, "Introduction: Desistance," in *Typography: Mimesis, Philosophy, Politics,* by Philippe Lacoue-Labarthe, ed. Christopher Fynsk (Stanford, Calif.: Stanford University Press, 1998), 1–42.

43. See Sauvanet, *Le Rythme grec,* 79.

44. Lacoue-Labarthe, "Echo of the Subject," 174, cit. in Derrida, "Introduction," 35.

45. Lacoue-Labarthe, "Echo of the Subject," 145.

46. Lacoue-Labarthe, 175.

47. Lacoue-Labarthe, 200.

48. See Jane Gallop, "Lacan's Mirror Stage: Where to Begin," *Substance* 11, no. 4 (1983): 121.

49. Jean Epstein, "The Fluid World of the Screen," in *Jean Epstein: Critical Essays and New Translations,* ed. Sarah Keller and Jason N. Paul (Amsterdam: Amsterdam University Press, 2012), 392; a note specifies that "the CGS system is a system of physical measures with the centimeter, the gram, and the second (CGS) as its basic units." For Epstein, cinema can resist and indeed undo the logic of

identity—which he clearly associates with a privilege of solid objects—that has historically marked our relationship to reality.

50. Roland Barthes, *How to Live Together*, trans. Kate Briggs (New York: Columbia University Press, 2012), 35.

51. In "Renoir's Automaton, Vigo's Puppet: Automatism and Movement in *La Règle du jeu* and *L'Atalante*," *French Studies* 70, no. 4 (2016): 547, Patrick Ffrench speaks of "polymorphous and exotic sexuality."

52. Virginia Woolf, *A Room of One's Own* (New York: Harcourt Brace, 1929), 38.

53. While celebrating the camera's capacity to produce a "liquefaction" of the visible world on behalf of the human eye, Epstein writes, "This eye sometimes becomes like a multifaceted fixed eye; sometimes like a multiplicity of eyes, each of which possesses a unique perspective; sometimes like a mobile snail eye, an eye mounted on an extendable and retractable stem." Jean Epstein, "Fluid World of the Screen," 383. On Anita Conti's photographs of life at sea, see Allan Sekula, "Between the Net and the Deep Blue Sea (Rethinking the Traffic in Photographs)," *October* 102 (2002): 3–34.

54. Like the waltz, a variation of the bargemen's song, the sound of the accordion now emerges in a zone of radical ambiguity between the diegetic and the non-diegetic.

55. Barthes, *How to Live Together*, 38.

56. Irigaray, "Volume without Contours," 56. I speak of rhuthmos whereas Irigaray speaks of "(the/a) woman."

57. Lacoue-Labarthe, "Echo of the Subject," 175.

58. Lacoue-Labarthe, 199.

59. Actually, the retreat has already begun in the previous section when he writes "between beat and figure" (Lacoue-Labarthe, 202), thus substituting Benveniste's rhuthmos with its measured counterpart.

60. Derrida, "Introduction," 34. His suggestion that only "a gap or a hiatus," "an arrhythmic caesura" (35), will interrupt this alternation in turn poses the problem of interruption mentioned below.

61. Lacoue-Labarthe, "Echo of the Subject," 175.

62. Irigaray, "Volume without Contours," 66.

63. Derrida, "Introduction," 34.

64. Lacoue-Labarthe, "Echo of the Subject," 199.

65. Irigaray, "'Mechanics' of Fluids," 115.

66. See Domietta Torlasco, "Against House Arrest: Antigone and the Impurity of the Death Drive," in *The Heretical Archive: Digital Memory at the End of Film* (Minneapolis: University of Minnesota Press, 2013), 1–24.

67. Giorgio Agamben, "Nymphs," trans. Amanda Minervini, in *Releasing the Image: From Literature to New Media*, ed. Jacques Khalip and Robert Mitchell (Stanford, Calif.: Stanford University Press, 2011), 75.

68. Agamben, 61.

69. Gilles Deleuze, *Cinema 2: The Time-Image*, trans. Hugh Tomlinson and Robert Galeta (Minneapolis: University of Minnesota Press, 1989), xi. On the complexity of stillness in dance, the difference between classical ballet's "held postures" and vibration dance in modern dance, see Lucia Ruprecht, "Gesture, Interruption, Vibration: Rethinking Early Twentieth-Century Gestural Theory and Practice in Walter Benjamin, Rudolf von Laban, and Mary Wigman," *Dance Research Journal* 47, no. 2 (2015): 23–42. Interestingly, she stresses the survival of an aesthetics of "wishful bodies" in Warburg at the same time that modern dance was being disturbed by "alien bodies" (25).

70. Agamben, "Nymphs," 62.

71. Henri Bergson, *The Creative Mind: An Introduction to Metaphysics*, trans. Mabelle L. Andison (Mineola, N.Y.: Dover, 1946), 3.

72. Roland Barthes, *Camera Lucida: Reflections on Photography*, trans. Richard Howard (New York: Hill and Wang, 2010), 115–16.

73. Agamben, "Nymphs," 74.

74. Agamben, 78.

75. On gesture as a "third type of action" that "breaks with the false alternative between ends and means" and is "endured and supported," see Giorgio Agamben, "Notes on Gesture," in *Means without End: Notes on Politics*, trans. Cesare Casarino and Vincenzo Binetti (Minneapolis: University of Minnesota Press, 2000), 57.

76. Irigaray, "Volume without Contours," 59.

77. Giorgio Agamben, "Difference and Repetition: On Guy Debord's Films," trans. Brian Holmes, in *Guy Debord and the Situationist International: Texts and Documents*, ed. Tom McDonough (Cambridge, Mass.: MIT Press, 2004), 313–19. For a reading of Agamben's work that explores but does not criticize its logic of interruption, see Nico Baumbach, "Cinema as Emergency Brake: Agamben and the Philosophy of Media after Benjamin," in *Cinema/Politics/Philosophy* (New York: Columbia University Press, 2019), 128–69.

78. Giorgio Agamben, *The Use of Bodies*, trans. Adam Kotsko (Stanford, Calif.: Stanford University Press, 2016), 172.

79. Lacoue-Labarthe, "Echo of the Subject," 201.

80. Agamben, *Use of Bodies*, 173.

81. See Martin Heidegger and Eugen Fink, *Heraclitus Seminar*, trans. Charles H. Seibert (Evanston: Northwestern University Press, 1997), 55, and

Martin Heidegger, *On the Way to Language*, trans. Peter D. Hertz (New York: Harper & Row, 1971), 149.

82. Werner Jaeger, *Paideia: The Ideals of Greek Culture, Volume I: Archaic Greece / The Mind of Athens*, 2nd ed., trans. Gilbert Highet (Oxford, UK: Oxford University Press, 1945), 126.

83. Agamben, *Use of Bodies*, 173 (emphasis mine).

84. Andrew Benjamin, "Spacing as the Shared: Heraclitus, Pindar, Agamben," in *Politics, Metaphysics, and Death: Essays on Giorgio Agamben's "Homo Sacer,"* ed. Andrew Norris (Durham, N.C.: Duke University Press, 2005), 167, cit. in Ewa Plonowska Ziarek, *Feminist Aesthetics and the Politics of Modernism* (New York: Columbia University Press, 2012), 143.

85. Ewa Plonowska Ziarek, "Feminine 'I can': On Possibility and Praxis in Agamben's Work," *Theory and Event* 13, no. 1 (2010).

86. Giorgio Agamben, "Form-of-Life," trans. Cesare Casarino, in *Radical Thought in Italy: A Potential Politics*, ed. Paolo Virno and Michael Hardt (Minneapolis: University of Minnesota Press, 1996), 150.

87. On vibration and gesture as "restless stillness" and an "aesthetic of *vibrant interruption*" in Benjamin, see Ruprecht, "Gesture, Interruption, Vibration"; for a reading of the temporality of the standstill that does not sever it from flow, see Samuel Weber, "Between a Human Life and a Word: Walter Benjamin and the Citability of Gesture," in *Perception and Experience in Modernity*, ed. Helga Geyer-Ryan (Amsterdam: Rodopi, 2002), 26–45.

88. Walter Benjamin, "Was ist das epische Theater? (I)," in *Gesammelte Schriften II: Aufsätze, Essays, Vorträge* (Frankfurt am Main: Suhrkamp Verlag, 1991), 531, cit. in Ruprecht, 27.

2. LABOR

1. Jean-Louis Comolli, "Mechanical Bodies, Ever More Heavenly," *October* 83 (1998): 19.

2. Comolli, 19. Simon's film is about a catering firm preparing fresh meals for large supermarkets.

3. Harun Farocki, "Workers Leaving the Factory," in *Harun Farocki: Working on the Sight-Lines*, ed. Thomas Elsaesser (Amsterdam: Amsterdam University Press, 2004), 238. See also Harun Farocki, "Workers Leaving the Factory," *Nachdruck/Imprint: Texte/Writings*, ed. Susanne Gaensheimer and Nicolaus Schafhausen (Berlin: Verlag Vorwerk, 2001), 230–48.

4. Apropos of this turning away from the space of production, see Hito Steyerl, "Is the Museum a Factory?," in *The Wretched of the Screen* (Berlin: Sternberg

Press, 2012). Steyerl, writing from the perspective of post-Fordism, recognizes that the workers leaving the factory were already on their way to do another kind of work. Overall, her essay is devoted to exploring the transition from cinema in the city to "cinema in the museum"—from a screening space that resembles the enclosed, highly structured space of the industrial factory to the space of the museum as one that approximates the "dispersed space of the social factory" (66).

5. Harun Farocki, *Weiche Montagen / Soft Montages*, ed. Yilmaz Dziewior (Bregenz: Kunsthaus Bregenz, 2010), 104 (emphasis mine).

6. Farocki, 104. See Maurizio Lazzarato, "Immaterial Labor," for a notion of productive labor that includes "the informational and cultural content of the commodity." In *Radical Thought in Italy: A Potential Politics*, ed. Paolo Virno and Michael Hardt (Minneapolis: University of Minnesota Press, 1996), 133.

7. See Kathi Weeks, *The Problem with Work: Feminism, Marxism, Antiwork Politics, and Postwork Imaginaries* (Durham, N.C.: Duke University Press, 2011).

8. Gilles Deleuze, "Postscript on the Societies of Control," *October* 59 (1992): 3.

9. Cesare Casarino, "Images for Housework: On the Time of Domestic Labor in Gilles Deleuze's Philosophy of the Cinema," *differences* 28, no. 3 (2017): 67–92. For Casarino, the theory of expression that Deleuze develops in his work on Spinoza will influence the cinema books "to the extent that it enables him to theorize the cinema at once as 'medium of expression' (rather than merely as medium of representation) and as 'expression of time'" (89).

10. See Domietta Torlasco, "Philosophy in the Kitchen," *World Picture* 11 (2016): http://worldpicturejournal.com/WP_11/Torlasco_11; on this video essay, see Olivia Landry and Christina Landry, "Torlasco's 'Philosophy in the Kitchen': Image, Domestic Labor, and the Gendered Embodiment of Time," *New Review of Film and Television Studies* 17, no. 4 (2019): 456–80.

11. See Patricia Pisters, "The Filmmaker as Metallurgist: Political Cinema and World Memory," *Film-Philosophy* 20, no. 1 (2016): 149–67.

12. Ivone Margulies, "Nothing Happens: Time for the Everyday in Postwar Realist Cinema," in *Nothing Happens: Chantal Akerman's Hyperrealist Everyday* (Durham, N.C.: Duke University Press, 1996), 21–41.

13. In addition to Weeks, see Cristina Morini, "The Feminization of Labour in Cognitive Capitalism," *Feminist Review* 87 (2007): 40–59.

14. Christian Marazzi, "Rules for the Incommensurable," *Substance* 36, no. 1 (2007): 21.

15. Marazzi, 17–19 (emphasis in original).

16. See Mariarosa Dalla Costa and Selma James, *The Power of Women and the Subversion of Community* (Bristol, UK: Falling Wall, 1973).

17. Michael Hardt and Antonio Negri, *Commonwealth* (Cambridge, Mass.: Harvard University Press, 2009), 132.

18. Michael Hardt and Antonio Negri, *Empire* (Cambridge, Mass.: Harvard University Press, 2000), 357. They write, "Whereas 'outside measure' refers to the impossibility of power's calculating and ordering production at a global level, 'beyond measure' refers to the vitality of the productive context, the expression of labor as desire, and its capacities to constitute the biopolitical fabric of Empire from below."

19. Marazzi, "Rules for the Incommensurable," 17.

20. See Annette Michelson, "Introduction," in *Kino-Eye: The Writings of Dziga Vertov*, trans. Kevin O'Brien (Berkeley: University of California Press, 1984).

21. Luisa Muraro, *Maglia o uncinetto: Racconto linguistico sull'inimicizia tra metafora e metonomia* (Milan: Feltrinelli, 1981). Selections from the book have been translated and published as a long essay, "To Knit or to Crochet: A Political-Linguistic Tale on the Enmity between Metaphor and Metonymy," in *Another Mother: Diotima and the Symbolic Order of Italian Feminism*, ed. Cesare Casarino and Andrea Righi, trans. Mark William Epstein (Minneapolis: University of Minnesota Press, 2018), 67–120. At the beginning of this work, Muraro explains that speaking is like knitting inasmuch as it requires the mobilization of the two axes of language (selection/substitution and combination).

22. I am thinking, for instance, of Christa Blümlinger's straightforward reliance on both rational and irrational intervals in "Memory and Montage: On the Installation *Counter-Music*," in *Harun Farocki: Against What? Against Whom?*, ed. Antje Ehmann and Kodwo Eshun (Cologne: Walter König, 2010), 101–9.

23. Kaja Silverman and Harun Farocki, *Speaking about Godard* (New York: New York University Press, 1998), 142.

24. Gilles Deleuze, *Cinema 2: The Time-Image*, trans. Hugh Tomlinson and Robert Galeta (Minneapolis: University of Minnesota Press, 1997), 180.

25. In *Cinema 2*, Deleuze writes, "For, in Godard's method, it is not a question of association. Given one image, another image has to be chosen which will induce an interstice *between* the two. This is not an operation of association, but of differentiation, as mathematicians say, or of disappearance, as physicists say: given one potential, another one has to be chosen, not any whatever, but in such a way that a difference of potential is established between the two, which will be productive of a third or of something new" (179).

26. Among the otherwise valuable contributions I criticize in this respect, see Nora Alter's reading of Godard in *The Essay Film after Fact and Fiction* (New York: Columbia University Press, 2017).

27. Gilles Deleuze, *Negotiations*, trans. Martin Joughin (New York: Columbia

University Press, 1997), 45. While answering a question about the television series *Six fois deux*, Deleuze is already articulating his theory of the interstice, which will later become operative in relation to Godard's cinema tout court.

28. Deleuze, *Cinema 2*, 180.

29. This happens prominently in Blümlinger, "Memory and Montage."

30. Gilles Deleuze, *Cinema 1: The Movement-Image*, trans. Hugh Tomlinson and Barbara Habberjam (Minneapolis: University of Minnesota Press, 2001), 82; Deleuze, *Cinema 2*, 180. Deleuze refers to the mathematical use of the terms "rational" and "irrational." On Vertov and mathematics, see also Anne Michelson, "The Wings of Hypothesis: On Montage and the Theory of the Interval," in *Montage and Modern Life: 1919–1942*, ed. Michael Teitelbaum (Cambridge, Mass.: MIT Press, 1992), 60–81.

31. Harun Farocki, "Cross Influence/Soft Montage," in *Harun Farocki: Against What? Against Whom?*, ed. Antje Ehmann and Kodwo Eshun (Cologne: Walter König, 2010), 70.

32. It is worth noting that Metz rightly prefers to speak of "operations" or "acts" rather than "figures," as the latter are often hybrid or composite.

33. The distinction between "positional" and "semantic" is key in this respect: Metz's distinction between paradigm/syntagm and metaphor/metonymy generates the possibility of four "main types of textual concatenation" (189): metaphor presented syntagmatically (*both* the flock of sheep *and* the crowd in the opening of Chaplin's *Modern Times*); metaphor presented paradigmatically (*= either-or*); metonymy presented paradigmatically (the child's balloon in Lang's *M*); and metonymy presented syntagmatically (*both* the child *and* the balloon). See Christian Metz, *The Imaginary Signifier: Psychoanalysis and the Cinema*, trans. Celia Britton (Bloomington: Indiana University Press, 1986).

34. Deleuze, *Cinema 2*, 214.

35. On the essayistic qualities of soft montage, see Rick Warner, "Essaying the Forms of Popular Cinema: Godard, Farocki, and the Principle of Shot/Countershot," in *The Film Essay: Dialogue, Politics, Utopia*, ed. Elizabeth Papazian and Caroline Eades (New York: Columbia University Press, 2016), 28–68.

36. Metz, *Imaginary Signifier*, 201.

37. Muraro, "To Knit or to Crochet," 72.

38. Muraro, 76.

39. Muraro, 71. See also Jacques Derrida, "White Mythology: Metaphor in the Text of Philosophy," in *Margins of Philosophy*, trans. Alan Bass (Chicago: University of Chicago Press, 1982), 207–71.

40. Muraro, 76.

41. Casarino, "Images for Housework," 85.

42. André Bazin, "*Umberto D.*: A Great Work," in *What Is Cinema? Volume II*, trans. Hugh Gray (Berkeley, Calif.: University of California Press, 1971), 81.

43. Giorgio Agamben, *Means without End: Notes on Politics*, trans. Vincenzo Binetti and Cesare Casarino (Minneapolis: University of Minnesota Press, 2000), 57. Casarino also distinguishes between "being exhausted" and "being tired" by referring to Deleuze's essay on Samuel Beckett: "the tired person has merely exhausted the realization, whereas the exhausted person exhausts the whole of the possible." Gilles Deleuze, "The Exhausted," *Essays Critical and Clinical*, trans. Michael A. Greco and Daniel W. Smith (Minneapolis: University of Minnesota Press, 1997), 152–53.

44. André Bazin, "Vittorio De Sica: Metteur en scène," in *What Is Cinema? Volume II*, 76.

45. Casarino, "Images for Housework," 86 (my emphasis).

46. Giorgio Agamben, *Potentialities: Collected Essays in Philosophy*, ed. and trans. Daniel Heller-Roazen (Stanford, Calif.: Stanford University Press, 1999), 179. For a discussion of the tension between Bartleby and Akhmatova, see Ewa Plonowska Ziarek, "Feminine 'I can': On Possibility and Praxis in Agamben's Work," *Theory and Event* 13, no. 1 (2010): https://doi.org/10.1353/tae.0.0109.

47. Roland Barthes, *How to Live Together*, trans. Kate Briggs (New York: Columbia University Press, 2013), 35.

48. Barthes, 8.

49. Muraro, "To Knit or to Crochet," 72.

50. Jonathan Crary, *24/7: Late Capitalism and the Ends of Sleep* (New York: Verso, 2013), 110, 126–27.

51. Deleuze, *Cinema 2*, 3.

52. Giorgio Agamben, *Infancy and History: On the Destruction of Experience*, trans. Liz Heron (Brooklyn, N.Y.: Verso, 2007), 99.

53. Awakening returns three times but, by virtue of rhythm, each cluster is already self-differing.

54. For Daney, "the visual knows no reverse shot [*contrechamp*], it lacks nothing, it is complete within itself, a closed circuit," while the image is always other than itself, "both more and simultaneously also less than what it is in itself." Originally drawn from Serge Daney's essay "Montage Obligatory: The War, the Gulf and the Small Screen," *Rouge* 8 (1991): http://www.rouge.com.au/8/montage.html, this passage appears in Farocki, *Soft Montages*, 65, and is re-cited in Warner, "Essaying the Forms of Popular Cinema," 52. See also Martin Blumenthal-Barby, "*Counter-Music*: Harun Farocki's Theory of a New Image Type," *October* 151 (2015): 128–50. In all cases, Vertov remains the primary point of reference, with Blumenthal-Barby claiming that "*Counter-Music* links the thematized history

of weaving with the history of seeing" and their decreasing dependency on human beings, but also pointing out a break in the means through which this analogy is pursued (137).

55. See Walter Benjamin, "The Work of Art in the Age of Its Technological Reproducibility: Second Version," in *The Work of Art in the Age of Its Technological Reproducibility and Other Writings on Media*, ed. Michael William Jennings, Brigid Doherty, and Thomas Y. Levin, trans. Edmund Jephcott et al. (Cambridge, Mass.: Belknap Press, 2006), 19–55.

56. Ivone Margulies, "The Equivalence of Events: *Jeanne Dielman, 23, Quai du Commerce, 1080 Bruxelles*," in *Nothing Happens: Chantal Akerman's Hyperrealist Everyday* (Durham, N.C.: Duke University Press, 1996), 65, 92.

57. André Bazin, "The Stylistics of Robert Bresson," in *What Is Cinema? Volume II*, trans. Hugh Gray (Berkeley: University of California Press, 1971), 131.

58. Margulies, "Equivalence of Events," 76.

59. Rosalind Krauss, "LeWitt in Progress," *October* 6 (1978): 60.

60. Margulies, "Equivalence of Events," 67.

61. Margulies, 96.

62. Krauss, "LeWitt in Progress," 55–56.

63. Jean-Joseph Goux, *Symbolic Economies: After Marx and Freud*, trans. Jennifer Curtiss Gage (Ithaca, N.Y.: Cornell University Press, 1990); Luce Irigaray, "Women on the Market," in *This Sex Which Is Not One*, trans. Catherine Porter and Carolyn Burke (Ithaca, N.Y.: Cornell University Press, 1985), 170–91.

64. On Mary Wigman's vibrato, see Lucia Ruprecht, "Gesture, Interruption, Vibration: Rethinking Early Twentieth-Century Gestural Theory and Practice in Walter Benjamin, Rudolf von Laban, and Mary Wigman," *Dance Research Journal* 47, no. 2 (2015): 23–42; see the discussion on the vibrating image at the end of chapter 1.

65. Judith Mayne writes, "There may not be an exact and identifiable cause for the murder of Jeanne's client, but the threat of randomness, of an interruption which is not immediately regulated and defined within cycles of repetition and ritual, looms over the film from the outset." Judith Mayne, *The Woman at the Keyhole: Feminism and Women's Cinema* (Bloomington: Indiana University Press, 1990), 205.

66. Akerman qtd. in Margulies, "Equivalence of Events," 96.

67. Silverman and Farocki, *Speaking about Godard*, 146–47, 161.

68. Luce Irigaray, "This Sex Which Is Not One," in *This Sex Which Is Not One*, trans. Catherine Porter and Carolyn Burke (Ithaca: Cornell University Press, 1985), 24.

69. Muraro, "To Knit or to Crochet," 113.

70. Muraro, 92, 101.

71. Muraro, 104.

72. Muraro, 104.

73. Muraro, 115; see also Luisa Muraro, "On the Relation between Words and Things as Frequentation," in *Another Mother: Diotima and the Symbolic Order of Italian Feminism*, ed. Cesare Casarino and Andrea Righi, trans. Mark William Epstein (Minneapolis: University of Minnesota Press, 2018), 121–30.

74. Muraro, "To Knit or to Crochet," 73.

75. Muraro, "On the Relation between Words and Things," 125.

76. In addition to the ending, there are small deviations from this pattern (like when a shot of the grandmother sewing on the balcony appears only on the right), so that the sequence's texture remains irregular.

77. Deleuze defines Godard's "stammering" as "creative" and "a foreign use of language," in *Negotiations*, 37–38, 44.

78. Roman Jakobson, "Two Aspects of Language and Two Types of Aphasic Disturbances," in *On Language: Roman Jakobson,* ed. Linda Waugh and Monique Monville-Burston (Cambridge, Mass.: Harvard University Press, 1998), 125 (emphasis mine).

79. This is one of the reasons why Metz explicitly chooses to speak of "operations" rather than "figures," as the figures themselves will most often be hybrid.

80. Jakobson, "Two Aspects of Language," 125.

81. In the second prologue, the video monitor above plays clips of miscellaneous fiction films (Claude Sautet, martial arts, porno, Ingmar Bergman, etc.), while the one below shows TV news and documentary footage of a May Day rally. In *Speaking about Godard*, 145, Silverman reads the shift from the first to the second prologue as an example of Godard's "authorial divestiture," underscoring how the initial inscription "a film written and directed . . ." is later replaced by Sandrine's voice crediting the production to multiple names: "A.-M. Miéville and PJ.-L. Godard, with S. Battistella, P. Oudry, and others."

82. In addition to *Speaking about Godard,* see Kaja Silverman, "The Author as Receiver," *October* 96 (2001): 17–34.

3. MEMORY

1. Jean-Luc Godard, "Montage, mon beau souci," *Cahiers du Cinéma* 65 (1956): 30–31. This English translation is taken from "Montage, mon beau souci," in *Fine Cuts: The Art of European Film Editing*, by Roger Crittenden (Burlington, Vt.: Focal Press, 2006), 1.

2. Bernard Stiegler, *Technics and Time, 3: Cinematic Time and the Question of Malaise,* trans. Stephen Barker (Stanford, Calif.: Stanford University Press, 2011).

3. Bernard Stiegler, *Symbolic Misery, Volume 1: The Hyperindustrial Epoch*, trans. Barnaby Norman (Cambridge, UK: Polity Press, 2014), 2.

4. Bernard Stiegler, *For a New Critique of Political Economy*, trans. Daniel Ross (Cambridge, UK: Polity Press, 2010), 53.

5. See Gilles Deleuze and Félix Guattari, *A Thousand Plateaus: Capitalism and Schizophrenia*, trans. Brian Massumi (London: Athlone Press, 1987). For an overview of Stiegler's work on rhythm and its relation to changing conditions of production and consumption, see Bram Ieven, "The Forgetting of Aesthetics: Individuation, Technology, and Aesthetics in the Work of Bernard Stiegler," *New Formations* 77 (2012): 76–96.

6. Stiegler, *Symbolic Misery*, 19 (emphasis in original).

7. Stiegler, 60.

8. Stiegler, *Technics and Time, 3*, 26. For a straightforward reading of Stiegler's work on editing, see Patrick Crogan, "Editing and Individuation," *New Formations* 77 (2012): 97–110.

9. Stiegler, 12.

10. Stiegler, *Symbolic Misery*, 52–53.

11. Stiegler, *Technics and Time, 3*, 39.

12. Stiegler draws the term "transindividuation" from Gilbert Simondon's *On the Mode of Existence of Technical Objects*. See Gilbert Simondon, *On the Mode of Existence of Technical Objects*, trans. Cecile Malaspina and John Rogove (Minneapolis: University of Minnesota Press, 2016); for an introduction to Simondon's work that highlights those complexities of transindividuation underplayed or neglected by Stiegler, see Muriel Combes, *Gilbert Simondon and the Philosophy of the Transindividual* (Cambridge, Mass.: MIT Press, 2012).

13. Donna Haraway, "Tentacular Thinking: Anthropocene, Capitalocene, Chthulucene," in *Staying with the Trouble: Making Kin in the Chthulucene* (Durham, N.C.: Duke University Press, 2016), 30–57.

14. Stiegler, *Symbolic Misery*, 22.

15. I started to develop a critique of Stiegler's treatment of montage in my previous book, *The Heretical Archive: Digital Memory at the End of Film* (Minneapolis: University of Minnesota Press, 2013), but there the question of rhythm had not yet been broached.

16. See Martin Jay, "Experience without a Subject: Walter Benjamin and the Novel," in *The Actuality of Walter Benjamin*, ed. Laura Marcus and Lynda Nead (London: Lawrence & Wisehart, 1998), 194–211.

17. See chapter 1 for a detailed discussion of Émile Benveniste.

18. Hansen writes that auratic cinema "would not only fulfill a critical function but also a redemptive one, registering sediments of experience that are no

longer or not yet claimed by social and economic rationality, making them readable as emblems of a 'forgotten future.'" Miriam Hansen, "Benjamin, Cinema and Experience: 'The Blue Flower in the Land of Technology,'" *New German Critique* 40 (1987): 209.

19. A close reader of Benjamin, Hansen focuses on the vicissitudes of the auratic in modernity. For a reading of the aura that emphasizes the transition to postmodernity and global capitalism, see Lutz Koepnick, "Aura Reconsidered: Benjamin and Contemporary Visual Culture," in *Benjamin's Ghosts: Interventions in Contemporary Literary and Cultural Theory*, ed. Gerhard Richter (Stanford, Calif.: Stanford University Press, 2002), 95–120.

20. See Martin Jay, *Songs of Experience: Modern American and European Variations on a Universal Theme* (Berkeley: University of California Press, 2005).

21. See Hansen, "Benjamin, Cinema and Experience"; and Miriam Hansen, "Benjamin and Cinema: Not a One-Way Street," *Critical Inquiry* 25, no. 2 (1999): 306–43.

22. Walter Benjamin, "The Work of Art in the Age of Its Technological Reproducibility: Second Version," in *The Work of Art in the Age of Its Technological Reproducibility and Other Writings on Media*, ed. Michael William Jennings, Brigid Doherty, and Thomas Y. Levin, trans. Edmund Jephcott et al. (Cambridge, Mass.: Belknap Press, 2006), 23.

23. Benjamin, 32. For a discussion of the expression "the object in its veil," adopted by Benjamin to describe the auratic object, see Miriam Hansen, "Benjamin's Aura," *Critical Inquiry* 34, no. 2 (2008): 336–75.

24. Benjamin, 23.

25. Hansen, "Benjamin's Aura," 342.

26. Hansen remarks that "Benjamin's 'definition' of aura is the only passage in the artwork essay written in a rhythm approaching metric verse" (352). That this key passage evokes the rhythm of metric verse might be argued to further reveal the intimacy existing between the auratic and the rhythmic, but I will not end up connecting auratic rhythm and prosody per se.

27. Walter Benjamin, *The Origin of German Tragic Drama*, trans. John Osborne (New York: Verso, 2009), 28.

28. Benjamin, "Work of Art in the Age of Its Technological Reproducibility," 29.

29. Hansen, "Benjamin and Cinema," 338.

30. Walter Benjamin, "On Some Motifs in Baudelaire," in *Illuminations*, ed. Hannah Arendt, trans. Harry Zohn (New York: Schocken Books, 1968), 194.

31. Benjamin, 175.

32. Benjamin, 163.

33. Hansen, "Benjamin, Cinema and Experience," 310.

34. Benjamin, "On Some Motifs in Baudelaire," 188.

35. See Hansen, "Benjamin, Cinema and Experience."

36. See Hansen, "Benjamin's Aura."

37. See Walter Benjamin, "The Image of Proust," in *Illuminations,* ed. Hannah Arendt, trans. Harry Zohn (New York: Schocken Books, 1968), 201–16.

38. Philippe Lacoue-Labarthe, "The Echo of the Subject," in *Typography: Mimesis, Philosophy, Politics,* by Philippe Lacoue-Labarthe, ed. Christopher Fynsk (Stanford, Calif.: Stanford University Press, 1998), 200, 175.

39. Lacoue-Labarthe, 196.

40. Émile Benveniste, "The Notion of 'Rhythm' in Its Linguistic Expression," in *Problems in General Linguistics,* trans. Mary Elizabeth Meek (Coral Gables, Fla.: University of Miami Press, 1971), 287.

41. Theodor Reik, *Surprise and the Psychoanalyst: On the Conjecture and Comprehension of Unconscious Processes,* trans. Margaret M. Green (New York: Dutton, 1937), 119, cit. in Lacoue-Labarthe, "Echo of the Subject," 198.

42. Reik., cit. in Lacoue-Labarthe, "Echo of the Subject," 198.

43. John Mowitt, *Percussion: Drumming, Beating, Striking* (Durham, N.C.: Duke University Press, 2002), 4.

44. Mowitt, 9.

45. Mowitt, 25.

46. Mowitt, 124–27, 130.

47. Mowitt, 33.

48. That Benjamin (unlike Stiegler) was also a practitioner of montage, a collector of hybrid textual fragments, a thinker whose method mimics the procedures of cinematic writing not only complicates his stance on the subject but also confirms that questions of form—of historical forms—bear political significance. On the relation between object and method, see Eva Geulen, "Under Construction: Walter Benjamin's 'The Work of Art in the Age of Mechanical Reproduction,'" in *Benjamin's Ghosts: Interventions in Contemporary Literary and Cultural Theory,* ed. Gerhard Richter (Stanford, Calif.: Stanford University Press, 2002), 121–42.

49. Laura Mulvey, "*Le Mépris* (Jean-Luc Godard 1963) and Its Story of Cinema: A 'Fabric of Quotations,'" in *Godard's Contempt: Essays from the London Consortium,* ed. Colin MacCabe and Laura Mulvey (Malden, Mass.: Wiley-Blackwell, 2012), 225–37.

50. Jacques Aumont, "The Fall of the Gods: Jean-Luc Godard's *Le Mépris* (1963)," in *French Film: Texts and Contexts,* ed. Susan Hayward and Ginette Vincendeau (London: Routledge, 1990), 176.

51. See Harun Farocki and Kaja Silverman, *Speaking about Godard* (New York:

New York University Press, 1998) for a detailed reading of the film that resonates with my own.

52. Stéphane Mallarmé, *Oeuvres complètes* (Paris: Gallimard, 1945), 644, cit. in Lacoue-Labarthe, "Echo of the Subject," 140.

53. Benjamin, "On Some Motifs in Baudelaire," 188–89.

54. Walter Benjamin, "The Rainbow: A Dialogue on Fantasy," trans. Peter Fenves, in *The Messianic Reduction: Walter Benjamin and the Shape of Time,* by Peter Fenves (Stanford, Calif.: Stanford University Press, 2011), 248, 252.

55. Howard Caygill, *Walter Benjamin: The Colour of Experience* (London: Routledge, 1998), 11.

56. Benjamin, "Work of Art in the Age of Its Technological Reproducibility," 22. This assertion comes at the end of a passage celebrating film as the medium that promotes "the liquidation of the value of tradition in the cultural heritage" and thus also precipitates the disappearance of the aura. I read it in the context of Benjamin's convoluted treatment of antinomies.

57. Caygill, *Colour of Experience,* 102. Caygill's work on color and experience has been crucial to my understanding of Benjamin's early work. However, it must be noticed that Caygill insists on cinema's anti-auratic status.

58. Benjamin, *Origin of German Tragic Drama,* 45.

59. See Theodor W. Adorno, "On Jazz," trans. Jamie Owen Daniels, *Discourse* 12, no. 2 (1989–90): 45–69.

60. Angela McRobbie, "Dance and Social Fantasy," in *Gender and Generation,* ed. Angela McRobbie and Mica Nava (London: Macmillan, 1984), 144 (emphasis in original). See also Mowitt, *Percussion,* for a discussion of this intermittence in the context of the percussive model.

61. Walter Benjamin, "A Short Speech on Proust," translated in Hansen, "Benjamin, Cinema and Experience," 211.

62. Theodor Reik, *The Haunting Melody: Psychoanalytic Experiences in Life and Music* (New York: Farrar, Straus and Young, 1953), 253, cit. in Lacoue-Labarthe, "Echo of the Subject," 193.

63. Lacoue-Labarthe, 195.

64. See Jacques Derrida, "Introduction: Desistance," in *Typography: Mimesis, Philosophy, Politics,* by Philippe Lacoue-Labarthe, ed. Christopher Fynsk (Stanford, Calif.: Stanford University Press, 1998), 31.

65. Lacoue-Labarthe, "Echo of the Subject," 202, 206.

66. The bodily ego is defined as a "sack of skin" in Jean Laplanche, *Life and Death in Psychoanalysis,* trans. Jeffrey Mehlman (Baltimore: Johns Hopkins University Press, 1976), 81.

67. In *Symbolic Misery,* 25, Stiegler can only interpret the impersonal as neutral

and ultimately inauthentic (the echo of Heidegger's *Das Man*, "the They," repeatedly returns in his use of the term "one"). See for instance the following passage: "I realize that *every-one* knows the songs, me included. And that, as such, this 'every' is a 'one' rather than a 'we': I belong to this neutral, impersonal, and yet so intimate 'one'. This 'one' which is not, in the end, at least *not quite*, a 'we'. As though it were missing something. As though, in the time of temporal industrial objects, *we* were lacking" (emphasis in original).

68. The film strip is taken from the work of Yervant Gianikian and Angela Ricci Lucchi, who for decades practiced a kind of archeology of cinema by reframing and reediting footage of war and colonial expansion. See, for instance, their cycle of war films (1995–2004) and *From the Pole to the Equator* (1987), which explicitly takes on Italy's forgotten colonial past.

69. Amy Taubin, "Sync or Swim," *Artforum* 57, no. 2 (October 2018): 61.

70. André Bazin, "An Aesthetic of Reality: Neorealism," in *What Is Cinema? Volume II*, trans. Hugh Gray (Berkeley: University of California Press, 1971), 33.

71. Taubin, "Sync or Swim," 61.

72. See Stiegler's "invention *of* the human." Bernard Stiegler, *Technics and Time, 1: The Fault of Epimetheus*, trans. Richard Beardsworth and George Collins (Stanford, Calif.: Stanford University Press, 1998), 137.

73. David Batchelor, *Chromophobia* (London: Reaktion Books, 2001), 22–23. On color and cinema, see Brian Price, "Color, the Formless, and Cinematic Eros," *Framework* 47, no. 1 (2006): 22–25.

74. Batchelor, 23.

75. Maurice Merleau-Ponty, *The Visible and the Invisible*, trans. Alphonso Lingis (Evanston, Ill.: Northwestern University Press, 1968), 132.

76. Merleau-Ponty, 134.

77. Together with clips of Arabian nights and thieves of Bagdad, we find images from classic Arab cinema, most notably Youssef Chahine's *Jamila, the Algerian* (1958) and more recent films such as Moufida Tlatli's *The Silences of the Palace* (1994) and Leyla Bouzid's *As I Open My Eyes* (2015). There is even time for sketching a story on the fictional Gulf state of Dofa. See Andréa Picard, "*The Image Book* (Jean-Luc Godard, Switzerland/France)—Masters," *Cinema Scope* 75 (2018): https://cinema-scope.com/cinema-scope-online/the-image-book-jean-luc-godard-switzerland-france-masters/.

78. See Le Corbusier, *Journey to the East*, trans. Ivan Žaknić (Cambridge, Mass.: MIT Press, 2007). In accordance with what I argue in chapter 2, I speak here of differentiation and not collision, as Georges Didi-Huberman does in his reading of Godard's "montage-image." While I share his emphasis on the constitutive plurality of the image, I am interested in montage for its ontological force rather than its

"knowledge value" (120), its indeterminate potential rather than its readability as understood by Didi-Huberman. In other words, I mobilize here my interpretation of rhuthmos as auratic constellation in place of his interpretation of the dialectical image. See Georges Didi-Huberman, *Images in Spite of All: Four Photographs from Auschwitz,* trans. Shane B. Lillis (Chicago: University of Chicago Press, 2008).

79. Jean-Luc Nancy, *Being Singular Plural,* trans. Robert D. Richardson and Anne E. O'Byrne (Stanford, Calif.: Stanford University Press, 2000), 84.

80. Nancy, 18.

81. See Giorgio Agamben, "Cinema and History: On Jean-Luc Godard," in *Cinema and Agamben: Ethics, Biopolitics and the Moving Image,* ed. Henrik Gustafsson and Asbjørn Grønstad (New York: Bloomsbury, 2014), 25–26, in which Agamben repeats his argument on Guy Debord almost verbatim.

4. MEDIUM

1. Sergei M. Eisenstein, "Piranesi, or the Fluidity of Forms," in *The Sphere and the Labyrinth: Avant-Gardes and Architecture from Piranesi to the 1970s,* by Manfredo Tafuri, trans. Pellegrino d'Acierno and Robert Connolly (Cambridge, Mass.: MIT Press, 1987), 65.

2. Eisenstein, 67.

3. Eisenstein, 70.

4. Eisenstein, 69.

5. Manfredo Tafuri, *The Sphere and the Labyrinth: Avant-Gardes and Architecture from Piranesi to the 1970s,* trans. Pellegrino d'Acierno and Robert Connolly (Cambridge, Mass.: MIT Press, 1987), 57.

6. First printed in Vladimir Nizhniĭ, *Lessons with Eisenstein* (New York: Hill & Wang, 1962), 124, cit. in Tafuri, *Sphere and the Labyrinth,* 56.

7. Luka Arsenjuk, *Movement, Action, Image, Montage: Sergei Eisenstein and the Cinema in Crisis* (Minneapolis: University of Minnesota Press, 2018), 5.

8. Arsenjuk, 140–41.

9. Even in the "dialectical image," which Arsenjuk distinguishes from the "symbolic image" and posits as a "response to time as division," (152) temporal multiplicity is conceived in terms of an either/or logic.

10. While introducing Eisenstein's "Montage and Architecture," Yve-Alain Bois returns to Piranesi in order to highlight the "decentering effect of parallax." Piranesi's etchings rupture the central space of the baroque with such force that the spectator is denied a stable point of reference, in space as well in time. However, Bois does not discuss how Eisenstein responds to the effects of too radical a crisis of unity. See Sergei M. Eisenstein and Yve-Alain Bois, "Montage and Architecture," trans. Michael Glenny, *Assemblage* 10 (1989): 111–15.

11. See Sergei Eisenstein, "Laocoön" and "[Rhythm]," in *Towards a Theory of Montage: Sergei Eisenstein Selected Works, Volume 2*, ed. Richard Taylor and Michael Glenny, trans. Michael Glenny (London: IB Tauris, 2010), 109–203 and 227–49.

12. Eisenstein, "[Rhythm]," 238.

13. Paolo Virno, *A Grammar of the Multitude: For an Analysis of Contemporary Forms of Life*, trans. Isabella Bertoletti, James Cascaito, and Andrea Casson (Cambridge, Mass.: Semiotext[e], 2003), 22.

14. Jacob Proctor, ed., *Victor Burgin: Prairie* (Chicago: University of Chicago Press, 2015), exhibition brochure. For a brilliant reading of Burgin's loops in relation to Henri Bergson's work, see Homay King, *Virtual Memory: Time-Based Art and the Dream of Digitality* (Durham, N.C.: Duke University Press, 2015).

15. See Jean Laplanche and Jean-Bertrand Pontalis, *The Language of Psycho-Analysis*, trans. Donald Nicholson-Smith (New York: W. W. Norton, 1973).

16. Sandro Mezzadra and Brett Neilson, *Border as Method, or, The Multiplication of Labor* (Durham, N.C.: Duke University Press, 2013), 151.

17. Étienne Balibar, "Uprisings in the Banlieues," *Constellations* 14, no. 1 (2007): 57 (emphasis in original).

18. See Mezzadra and Nielsen, *Border as Method*, 154.

19. My focus on "narrative" is far from being mutually exclusive with an acknowledgment of the role played by various administrative techniques, aggressive policing, and mass incarceration. See Simone Brown, *Dark Matters: On the Surveillance of Blackness* (Durham, N.C.: Duke University Press, 2015); and Michelle Alexander, *The New Jim Crow: Mass Incarceration in the Age of Color Blindness* (New York: New Press, 2010).

20. Étienne Balibar, "What Is a Border?," in *Politics and the Other Scene*, trans. Christine Jones, James Swenson, and Chris Turner (New York: Verso, 2002), 76.

21. Roland Barthes, *How to Live Together: Novelistic Simulations of Some Everyday Spaces*, trans. Kate Briggs (New York: Columbia University Press, 2013), 133.

22. Peter Osborne, "Photography in an Expanding Field: Distributive Unity and Dominant Form," in *Where Is the Photograph?* ed. David Green (Brighton, UK: Photoworks/Photoforum, 2003), 69.

23. Roland Barthes, "Diderot, Brecht, Eisenstein," in *Image Music Text*, trans. Stephen Heath (New York: Hill & Wang, 1978), 72.

24. Denis Diderot, "Composition, en Peinture," in *Encyclopédie, ou dictionnaire raisonné des sciences, des arts et des métiers*, vol. 3 (Paris: André le Breton, Michel-Antoine David, Laurent Durand, and Antoine-Claude Briasson, 1753), 772, cit. and trans. in Barthes, 71.

25. Sergei Eisenstein, *Film Form: Essays in Film Theory*, ed. and trans. Jay Leyda

(New York: Harcourt Brace Jovanovich, 1977), 37, cit. in Tafuri, *Sphere and the Labyrinth*, 59.

26. Barthes, "Diderot, Brecht, Eisenstein," 73.

27. Barthes, 73. The heightened gestures performed by Bertolt Brecht's *Mother Courage* and the peasant woman in Eisenstein's *Старое и новое* (*The General Line*, 1929) stand at the center of a chain of events that is both chronological and causal.

28. Roland Barthes, "The Third Meaning," in *Image Music Text*, trans. Stephen Heath (New York: Hill & Wang, 1978), 53.

29. Barthes, 62, 64, 67.

30. Sergei Eisenstein, "Montage 1938," in *Towards a Theory of Montage: Selected Works*, ed. Michael Glenny and Richard Taylor, trans. Michael Glenny (London: IB Tauris, 2010), 298.

31. Barthes, "Third Meaning," 63.

32. On Chicago's clear-cut internal boundaries and race relations, see Douglass S. Massey and Nancy A. Denton, *American Apartheid: Segregation and the Making of the Underclass* (Cambridge, Mass.: Harvard University Press, 1993); and Robert J. Sampson, *Chicago and the Enduring Neighborhood Effect* (Chicago: University of Chicago Press, 2012). For an account of the early city planners' cartographic imagination, see Carl Smith, *The Plan of Chicago: Daniel Burnham and the Remaking of the American City* (Chicago: University of Chicago Press, 2006).

33. I am responding to Catherine Clément's statement that "there is no dance without syncope—without syncopation." See Catherine Clément, *Syncope: The Philosophy of Rapture*, trans. Sally O'Driscoll and Deidre M. Mahoney (Minneapolis: University of Minnesota Press, 1994), 2. On syncopation and subject formation, see chapter 3.

34. Gwendolyn Brooks, "In the Mecca," in *In the Mecca* (New York: Harper and Row, 1968), 5.

35. Cit. in Daniel Bluestone, "Chicago's Mecca Flat Blues," in *Giving Preservation a History: Histories of Historic Preservation in the United States*, ed. Max Page and Randall Mason (London: Routledge, 2004), 181.

36. See Stephen Heath, *Questions of Cinema* (Bloomington: Indiana University Press, 1981).

37. In *Reading in Detail: Aesthetics and the Feminine* (London: Routledge, 2007), 14, Naomi Schor quotes Lord Kames: "In gardening as well as in architecture, simplicity ought to be the governing taste. Profuse ornament hath no better effect than to confound the eye, and to prevent the object from making an impression as one entire whole. . . . Thus a woman who has no taste, is apt to overcharge every part of her dress with ornament."

38. Even in the case of longer exposures, what is assumed is a coincidence between the time of the *prise de vue* and the self-presence of what is being photographed. In fact, this assumption continues to characterize even Thierry De Duve's distinction between snapshot and time exposure. See De Duve, "Time Exposure and Snapshot: The Photograph as Paradox," *October* 5 (1978): 113–25.

39. D. N. Rodowick, "The Unnameable (in Three Movements)," in *Projective: Essays about the Work of Victor Burgin,* by Victor Burgin, Gülru Çakmak, David Campany, Homay King, and D. N. Rodowick (Geneva: Musée d'art moderne et contemporain, 2014), 9.

40. Victor Burgin, "Specificity," in *Components of a Practice* (Milan: Skira, 2008), 93. It is important to notice that here Burgin speaks of "the specificity of a practice" rather than of a medium per se.

41. Burgin, 91 (emphasis mine).

42. Victor Burgin, "The Eclipse of Time," in *Time and Photography,* ed. Jan Baetens, Alexander Streitberger, and Hilde Van Gelder (Leuven: Leuven University Press, 2010), 135. Working "beyond clock-time," as is the case in our neoliberal economy, does not entail having left behind the quantification of time; rather, it indicates a more intensive exploitation of the instant and its increasingly smaller subdivisions in order to produce an impression of natural continuity.

43. Jeff Wall, "Photography and Liquid Intelligence," in *Jeff Wall: Selected Essays and Interviews,* ed. Peter Galassi (New York: Museum of Modern Art, 2007), 110.

44. Burgin, "Specificity," 92.

45. On the incomputable and the role of contingency in algorithmic thought itself, see Luciana Parisi, *Contagious Architecture: Computation, Aesthetics, and Space* (Boston: MIT Press, 2013).

46. See Victor Burgin, "Uncinematic Time," in *Victor Burgin's "Parzival" in Leuven: Reflections on the "Uncinematic,"* ed. Stéphane Symons and Hilde van Gelder (Leuven: Leuven University Press, 2017), 76–88.

47. Arata Isozaki, *Japan-ness in Architecture,* ed. David B. Stewart, trans. Sabu Kohso (Cambridge, Mass.: MIT Press, 2011), 95.

48. Isozaki, 82.

49. Henri Lefebvre, *Rhythmanalysis: Space, Time, and Everyday Life,* trans. Gerald Moore and Stuart Elden (New York: Continuum, 2004), 5.

50. Lefebvre, 37, 40–41.

51. Victor Burgin, *The Remembered Film* (London: Reaktion Books, 2004), 21.

52. Burgin, 21.

53. Burgin, 14.

54. Barthes, *How to Live Together,* 9.

55. Barthes, 6, 8.

56. Barthes, 35.

57. Michel Foucault, "'Society Must Be Defended,' Lecture at the *Collège de France,* March 17, 1976," in *Biopolitics: A Reader,* ed. Timothy Campbell and Adam Sitze (Durham, N.C.: Duke University Press, 2013), 61–62.

58. Gilles Deleuze, *Foucault,* trans. Sean Hand (Minneapolis: University of Minnesota, 1995), 92.

59. For an elaboration of Agamben's notion of "form-of-life" in relation to rhuthmos, see the first chapter of this book.

60. Barthes, *How to Live Together,* 35.

61. Barthes, 114–16.

62. Ryan Bishop and Sean Cubitt, "Camera as Object and Process: An Interview with Victor Burgin," *Theory, Culture & Society* 30, nos. 7–8 (2013): 211.

63. Roland Barthes, *The Pleasure of the Text,* trans. Richard Miller (New York: Hill & Wang, 1975), 9–10.

64. Allan Sekula, *Photography against the Grain: Essays and Photo Works, 1973–1983* (London: Mack Books, 2016), 34. See also Mary Ann Doane, "Real Time: Instantaneity and the Photographic Imaginary," in *Stillness and Time: Photography and the Moving Image,* ed. David Green and Joanna Lowry (Brighton, UK: Photoworks/Photoforum, 2006), 23–39.

65. Rodowick, "Unnameable," 35.

66. Peter Osborne, "Photography in an Expanding Field: Distributive Unity and Dominant Form," in *Where Is the Photograph?,* ed. David Green (Brighton, UK: Photoworks/Photoforum, 2003), 68–69.

67. In "Reinventing the Medium," *Critical Inquiry* 25 (1999): 289–305, Rosalind Krauss argues that "the medium [James] Coleman seems to be elaborating is just this paradoxical collision between stillness and movement" (297), one that mobilizes the adoption of the slide tape as physical support. Here the medium is understood as "a set of conventions derived from (but not identical with) the material conditions of a given technical support" (296) and, as such, open to historical mutation. However, Krauss opposes the reinvention of photography as medium to the affirmation of its status as heterogeneous object. In contrast, I consider such heterogeneity (as it still emerges in Burgin's post-conceptual practice) the condition for the medium's renewal.

68. Sekula, *Photography against the Grain,* 34.

69. Paul Virilio, *War and Cinema: The Logistics of Perception,* trans. Patrick Camiller (New York: Verso, 1989), 4. See also Domietta Torlasco, "Impossible Photographs: Images of War from Rossellini to dOCUMENTA 13," *Discourse* 40, no. 1 (Winter 2018): 110–31. Here I also develop a rereading of Barthes's *punctum* in light of Jacques Derrida's critique of the referent as it appears in "The Deaths of

Roland Barthes," in *Philosophy and Non-Philosophy since Merleau-Ponty*, ed. Hugh J. Silverman (Evanston, Ill.: Northwestern University Press, 1988), 275.

70. Maurice Merleau-Ponty, "Working Notes," in *The Visible and the Invisible*, ed. Claude Lefort, trans. Alphonso Lingis (Evanston, Ill.: Northwestern University Press, 1968), 240.

71. See Jacques Derrida's critique of Marcel Proust and Paul Claudel in *Writing and Difference*, trans. Alan Bass (Chicago: University of Chicago Press, 1978).

72. Barthes, *How to Live Together*, 5.

73. Barthes, 133.

74. Naoki Sakai, *Translation and Subjectivity: On "Japan" and Cultural Nationalism* (Minneapolis: University of Minnesota Press, 1997), 7. Sakai is also a key figure in the final chapter of Mezzadra and Neilson's *Border as Method*, "Translating the Commons" (277–312), where his notion of heterolingual translation is opposed to Ernesto Laclau and Chantal Mouffe's concept of articulation.

75. Sakai, 122. Sakai calls this being-in-common "a *communism* in the sense specified by Jean-Luc Nancy," referring to Nancy's elaboration of the concept in *The Inoperative Community*, ed. Peter Connor (Minneapolis: University of Minnesota Press, 1991).

76. Sakai, 122, 124.

77. Rosalind Krauss, "The Im/Pulse to See," in *Vision and Visuality*, ed. Hal Foster (Seattle: Bay Press, 1988), 51–52.

78. Krauss, 51.

79. See Sigmund Freud, "A Child Is Being Beaten," *Journal of Nervous and Mental Disease* 56, no. 4 (1922): 405–6.

80. Krauss, "Im/Pulse to See," 63.

81. Aristotle's definition of the instant as a point within a serial succession, the very guarantee of cosmological time, entailed positing time as "the number of motion with respect of 'before' and 'after.'" See Peter Osborne, *Politics of Time: Modernity and Avant-Garde* (New York: Verso, 1995), 45.

82. The acronym EUR stands for Esposizione Universale Roma, a monumental project planned under Benito Mussolini to host the 1942 World's Fair (which never took place because of the war). The place also holds special relevance in Italian postwar cinema, appearing as a crucial location in films such as Roberto Rossellini's *Rome Open City* and Federico Fellini's *La Dolce Vita*, among others. See J. D. Rhodes, "The Eclipse of Place: Rome's EUR, from Rossellini to Antonioni," in *Taking Place: Location and the Moving Image*, ed. John David Rhodes and Elena Gorfinkel (Minneapolis: University of Minnesota Press, 2011), 31–54.

83. See Alessia Ricciardi, "Becoming Woman: From Antonioni to Anne Carson and Cindy Sherman," *Yearbook of Comparative Literature* 56 (2010): 6–23.

84. In the third volume of *Technics and Time*, Bernard Stiegler turns his attention to both Hitchcock's TV episode and Antonioni's film to underscore the coincidence between the time of the film and the time of the spectator's consciousness.

85. Seymour Chatman, *Antonioni, or, the Surface of the World* (Berkeley: University of California Press, 1985), 80.

86. See Osborne, *Politics of Time*, on the distinction between "time of the world" (Aristotle and the cosmological tradition) and "time of the soul" (Augustine and the phenomenological tradition).

87. See Paul Virilio, *The Great Accelerator*, trans. Julie Rose (Cambridge, Mass.: Polity, 2012).

88. In *Antonioni*, 81, Chatman claims that "not temporal succession but spatial coexistence becomes the guiding principle." However, he identifies this absence of temporal succession with atemporality tout court.

89. Krauss, "Reinventing the Medium," 296.

Index

Page numbers in italic refer to figures. Film titles are cited in their English-language translations.

Adorno, Theodor W., 90
Aeschylus, 131n29
aesthetics, 7, 22–23, 59, 73–74, 76, 84, 104, 118, 126, 134n69; of heterogeneity (Godard), 43; of homogeneity (Akerman), 43, 61; and politics, 5, 14, 22, 59, 74, 101
Agamben, Giorgio, 10–11, 54–55, 58; and nymphs, 19, 33–36; and phantasmata, 33–34, 74, 118; and rhuthmos, 6, 35–38
Akerman, Chantal, 5. See also *Jeanne Dielman, 23, Quai du Commerce, 1080 Bruxelles*
Akhmatova, Anna, 37, 55
Alexander Nevskyi (Eisenstein), 99
Antonioni, Michelangelo, 5. See also *Eclipse, The*
Archilochus, 131n29
Arendt, Hannah, 130n23
Aristotle, 20, 22, 125, 132n39, 152n81, 153n86. *See also* pre-Socratic philosophy
Arsenjuk, Luka, 101, 147n9
As I Open My Eyes (Bouzid), 146n77
Atalante, L' (Vigo), 11, 19, 24–33, 37–38, 96; stills from, *24, 25, 26*
At All Costs (*Coûte que coûte*, Simon), 39
Augustine, Saint, 153n86
Aumont, Jacques, 84
aura: in Benjamin, 11, 75–83, 87–88, 142n18, 143n22, 143n26, 144n48, 145n57; in Hansen's reading, 76–79, 91, 142n18, 143n19, 143n23, 143n26; and rhuthmos/rhythm, 11–12, 75–78, 80, 82, 87–88, 92, 143n26, 146n78

Bachelard, Gaston, 96, 114. See also *Water and Dreams*
Badalamenti, Angelo, 90

155

Balibar, Étienne, 103, 104
Barthes, Roland, 7, 29, 34, 68; *How to Live Together,* 55, 104–5, 115–17, 120; and idiorrhythmy, 27, 38; and rhuthmos, 4–6, 20, 27
Bataille, Georges, 2
Batchelor, David, 94
Battleship Potemkin, The (Eisenstein), 101
Baudelaire, Charles, 78, 86
Bazin, André, 53–55, 60, 83, 94
beat, 11, 12, 81–82, 93, 105, 133n59
Beckett, Samuel, 139n43
becoming, 9, 33; "becoming-ill" (Stiegler), 72; "becoming-one" (Stiegler), 73; fluidity's relationship to, 11, 15–16, 29, 66, 113, 129n5; and *narum,* 114; and origin (Benjamin), 88; and rhuthmos, 19, 22, 24–25. *See also* fluidity; potentiality
being, 35, 38, 152n75; "being-in-common" (Sakai), 121, 152n75; "colored being" (Merleau-Ponty), 95; and intermittence, 25–26, 31, 72, 90; mode of, 3–4, 16, 18–19, 26, 35–37, 102; as rhythm, 3–4, 7–8, 26; of subjects and objects, 7–8, 16, 65, 73, 87, 120. *See also* life; rhythm
Benjamin, Walter, 1, 3, 33, 35, 37, 59; artwork essay, 77–80, 88, 145n56–57; on aura, 11, 75–83, 87–88, 142n18, 143n22, 143n26, 144n48, 145n57; Baudelaire essay, 78, 86; Hansen's reading of, 76–80, 91, 143n19, 143n26; on memory, 81–82, 83
Benveniste, Émile, 4–7, 18–22, 35–36, 81, 115–16, 131nn29–30, 133n59
Bergman, Ingrid, 41

Bergson, Henri, 7, 34, 148n14
Berlin: Symphony of a City (*Berlin: Sinfonie einer Großstadt,* Schadt), 40
Berlin Express (Tourneur), 98
Bicycle Thieves (*Ladri di biciclette,* De Sica), 42, 58
Blade Runner (Scott), 1
Blumenthal-Barby, Martin, 139n54
Blythe, James, "Mecca Flat Blues," 110
body, 25, 32, 39, 97, 106; as configuration, 29, 51, 56, 62, 97, 113; and excess, 1, 3, 15, 23, 26, 87, 90, 94, 97; and rhuthmos/rhythm, 5, 19–23, 35, 72; and sexual difference, 15–16, 28, 51, 64–65. *See also* dance; gesture; movement: of bodies
Bois, Yve-Alain, 147n10
border, 1, 7, 12, 14, 16, 47, 57, 116, 149n32; and definition, 92, 104, 116; and race, 103, 148n19, 149n31; temporal, 103, 120. *See also* enclosure; frame
Bouzid, Leyla. See *As I Open My Eyes*
Brecht, Bertolt, 105, 149n27
Breton, André, 57
Brooks, Gwendolyn, "In the Mecca," 110
Burgin, Victor, 5, 12, 17, 150n40, 151n67. *See also Prairie*

cadence, 55–56, 78, 86, 115, 131n30
Casanova (Fellini), 34
Casarino, Cesare, 41–42, 51, 53–55, 136n9, 139n43
Caygill, Howard, 87, 88, 145n57
Cézanne, Paul, 9, 117
Chahine, Youssef. See *Jamila, the Algerian*

Chaplin, Charlie, 68. See also *Modern Times*
Chatman, Seymour, 125, 153n88
cinema: "acinematic" (Lyotard), 2; as apparatus/technology, 2, 11, 16, 38, 40, 68, 75, 78, 91, 129n4; as auratic medium, 76–80, 88, 91, 93, 142n18, 145n57; and consciousness, 34, 72–73, 92, 153n84; death of, 1, 83, 93; Deleuze's philosophy of, 11, 34, 42, 46–49, 58; and domestic labor, 41–42, 45, 53, 61, 63; and industrial labor, 39–40, 45, 65; memory of, 75, 79; and (optical) unconscious, 76, 78; and time/temporality, 10, 107, 126, 136n9, 153n84; "uncinematic" (Burgin), 112–14. See also editing; montage
city, 40–41, 43, 57, 58, 59, 103
Claudel, Paul, 95
Clément, Catherine, 82
Coleman, James, 151n67
color, 2, 87, 94, 97; configurations of, 12, 68–69, 74, 94, 96–97; and aura, 87; in Godard, 67, 83–88, *85*, 93–98; and line, 8, 94–96, 145n57; and race, 94–95
Comolli, Jean-Louis, 39–40
configuration, 3, 5, 19, 24, 36, 38, 74–75, 125–26; auratic, 86–88, 92; bodily, 3, 58, 60–61, 63–64, 68; chromatic, 12, 68–69, 74, 94, 96–97; fleeting/fugitive, 83, 104, 118–20; intermittent, 56, 87–88, 97, 117; of matter, 24, 29, 87, 111; rhuthmos as, 10, 18–20, 22, 29–30, 55–56, 69, 80, 104, 126; self-differing, 3, 24, 92, 103, 118. See also fluctuation

consciousness, 34, 72–75, 78, 84, 92, 153n84. See also subject; unconscious, the
Contempt (*Le Mépris*, Godard), 11–12, 75, 82–88, 95; stills from, *85*
Conti, Anita, 28
continuity, 3, 11, 15, 51, 54, 74, 78, 150n42. See also succession
Counter-Music (*Contre-chante*, Farocki), 11, 40, 43–51, 56–59, 139n54; stills from, *47*
Courbet, Gustave, 58
Coutard, Raoul, 83–88
Crary, Jonathan, 57–58
Crown Hall, Illinois Institute of Technology (Chicago), 102, *107*, 109–10

dance, 1–2, 110–11, 132n39, 134n69; in *Casanova*, 34; in *L'Atalante*, 19, 24, 24–33, *25*, *26*, 37–38, 96; in *Mulholland Drive*, 89–91; nymphal, 36–37; in Plato, 5, 19–24; in *Prairie*, *108*, 109. See also movement; music
Daney, Serge, 59, 139n54
Debord, Guy, 35, 37
Debussy, Claude, 9
De Duve, Thierry, 150n38
Delerue, Georges, 86
Deleuze, Gilles, 6, 11, 41–42, 48–49, 51–54, 58, 67, 72, 116, 129n5, 136n9, 139n43; on interstice/interval, 46–49, 137n25; movement-image, 33–34; time-image, 34, 42, 53. See also editing; montage
Democritus, 20
De Quincey, Thomas, 100

Derrida, Jacques, 10, 20, 23, 31–32, 132n42, 133n60
De Sica, Vittorio, 53–54. See also *Bicycle Thieves*; *Umberto D.*
Diagne, Souleymane Bachir, 7–9
Diderot, Denis, 106
Didi-Huberman, Georges, 146n78
difference, 2, 126, 130n20, 146n78; and identity, 9–10, 12, 24; radical/absolute, 3–4, 21; and rhuthmos/rhythm, 3–4, 6–7, 21, 32, 56, 75, 95, 114, 134n69; sexual, 20–21, 25–26, 33, 37, 43, 94; simultaneity as, 12, 21, 126. See also interstice; interval
discontinuity, 29, 37, 54–55, 91
Dolce Vita, La (Fellini), 152n82
Domenichino, 33–34, 37
dreams, 57, 76, 86–87, 91, 122. See also fantasy
duration, 5, 12, 34, 96, 109, 112–14, 119, 125–26; in De Sica, 42, 53–55
Dürer, Albrecht, 17

Earth Trembles, The (*La terra trema*, Visconti), 42
Eclipse, The (*L'Eclisse*, Antonioni), 12, 73, 105, 112, 123–26, 153n84; still from, *124*
economy, 2, 43–44, 125, 143n19
editing, 28, 48, 51, 56, 87, 93, 110; and consciousness (Stiegler), 11, 73–75, 92; in Farocki, 58–59, 63; housework and, 11, 54, 63–69. See also cinema; interstice; montage; soft montage
Eisenstein, Sergei, 7, 49; and montage, 106–7; Piranesi essay, 101, 102, 105, 120, 147n10; and rhythm, 99–103. See also *General Line, The*

Employees Leaving the Lumière Factory (*La sortie de l'usine Lumière à Lyon*, Lumière), 39
enclosure, 99–107, 109, 119, 121, 126. See also border; frame
Epstein, Jean, 26, 28, 132n49, 133n53
equivalence, 2, 37, 50–51, 60, 62, 66–67, 104, 121, 127n4. See also homogeneity; identity
erotics, 2–3, 29, 32, 122
Esposizione Universale Roma (EUR, Italy), 152n82
Europe '51 (*Europa '51*, Rossellini), 41
experience, 1, 7–8, 25–26, 43, 50–51, 56, 65, 91–92; in Benjamin, 75–80, 88, 113, 142n18; and color, 87, 97, 145n57

Fantastic Voyage (Fleischer), 59
fantasy, 81, 87, 102, 111, 120, 125–26; of life, 6, 27, 104–5, 115, 120; temporality of, 115, 120, 126
Farocki, Harun, 5, 16, 48–49, 58–59, 63–64. See also *Counter-Music*; *I Thought I Was Seeing Convicts*; *Workers Leaving the Factory*
Fellini, Federico. See *Casanova*; *Dolce Vita, La*; *Interview*
feminism, Italian, 7, 51. See also Muraro, Luisa
Fleischer, Richard. See *Fantastic Voyage*
flesh, 82, 98; Merleau-Ponty's ontology of, 2–3, 9–10, 95. See also body
flowing, 54, 73; form's opposition to, 11, 36, 37; "manner of," (Benveniste), 5, 18–24, 80, 103; See also rhuthmos: etymology of; water
fluctuation, 124; and form, 21, 96; as

Index

rhuthmos, 5–6, 10, 11, 31–32, 33, 37, 75, 96, 115
fluidity, 13–19, 33, 56, 113, 129n5, 129n11; and becoming, 1, 11, 15, 16. *See also* Irigaray, Luce
flux, 22, 73, 131n35; of being, 36. *See* flowing; fluidity
form, 2, 5–8, 33, 35–37, 75, 87, 114, 122, 144n48; as fluctuation, 21, 96; fluid, 17–19; of life, 3–4, 7, 11, 32–38, 63, 116; and matter, 4–5, 10, 14–15, 18–19, 24, 87, 97–98, 113, rhuthmos as, 18–24, 30–38, 55–56, 63, 80–81, 131n30; skhema as, 19–21, 23, 36
formalism, 8, 10, 37, 62
Foucault, Michel, 10, 116
frame, 46, 64, 68, 113, 116–17. *See also* borders; enclosure
Freud, Sigmund, 66, 84, 111. *See also* psychoanalysis
Fried, Michael, 121
Frobenius, Leo, 8

Gasché, Rodolphe, 20, 131n30
General Line, The (Eisenstein), 149n27
gesture, 34–36, 51, 54, 56, 59–60, 63, 134n75, 149n27
Gianikian, Yervant, 146n68
Girl Can't Help It, The (Tashlin), 89–90
Godard, Jean-Luc, 5; and color, 67–68, 94–98; Deleuze on, 49, 67, 137n27; and montage, 71–72, 146n78. *See also Contempt*; *Histoire(s) du cinema*; *Image Book, The*; *Number Two*; *Two or Three Things I Know about Her*
Goux, Jean-Joseph, 2, 62, 127n4
Greenberg, Clement, 121

Griffith, D. W., 49, 50, 68
Groddeck, Georg, 31
Guattari, Félix, 6, 20, 72, 129n5
Guillaume, Paul, 8

Hansen, Miriam, 75–80, 91, 142n18, 143n26
Haraway, Donna, 74
Hardt, Michael, 44, 137n18
Hayles, N. Katherine, 15–16, 129n11
heartbeat, 31, 71, 90, 92–93, 101, 124
Heath, Stephen, 111
Heidegger, Martin, 20, 36
Heraclitus, 22, 36, 131n35
heterogeneity, 6, 43, 74, 90, 120, 121, 129n5, 151n67
Histoire(s) du cinema (Godard), 93–94
Hitchcock, Alfred: "Four O'Clock," 124, 153n84. *See also Vertigo*
homogeneity, 8, 43, 61, 72. *See also* equivalence; identity
housework, 11, 41–45, 51–57, 63–69. See also *Jeanne Dielman, 23, Quai du Commerce, 1080 Bruxelles*; labor; *Umberto D.*
hydraulics, 15–16, 129n5, 130n18
hypermetaphoricity, 45, 50, 57, 65. *See also* metaphor

identity, 9, 102, 132n42, 132n49. *See also* equivalence; homogeneity; metaphor
idiorrhythmy, 6, 27, 38, 104, 105, 115–16, 120
Image Book, The (*Le Livre d'image*, Godard), 12, 93–94, 97
image(s), 1–2, 19, 25, 73, 86, 91, 113, 130n19; and becoming, 25, 29, 64, 113, 114; dialectical, 146n78,

147n9; difference within, 4, 12, 43, 95; digital, 94, 109, 113, 118; echo of, 86, 114–15; imageless cinema (Agamben), 34; as imago, 31–32, 82; and instantaneity, 12, 17–18, 105, 112, 126; life of, 1, 4, 10–11, 27, 33, 38; mirror, 6, 15–16, 23, 25, 28; movement-image, 34, 42, 49; as nymphs (Agamben), 19, 33–36; ontological force of, 25–26, 146n78; as rhuthmos, 24–26, 54; sound and, 13, 27, 76; specular, 23, 25, 29, 132n42; time-image, 34, 42, 53, 55. *See also* cinema; photography

Images of the World and the Inscription of War (*Bilder der Welt und Inschrift des Krieges,* Farocki), 11, 13–19, 129n4, 130n20

individuation, 72–73, 75, 142n12

instantaneity, 12, 17, 21, 112, 114, 119, 121–26, 152n81. *See also* time

interruption, 3, 54, 133n60; Agamben and, 34, 37, 38; power of, 35–36, 38

interstice, 47–49, 113–14, 137n25, 137n28. *See also* Deleuze, Gilles; difference; editing; montage

interval, 47, 49, 57, 59, 63, 71, 75, 92, 113–14, 137n22. *See also* interstice

Interview (*Intervista*, Fellini), 73

Irigaray, Luce, 6, 10, 32, 62; and becoming, 15–16, 25; and metonymy, 44, 66; science critique, 14–15, 16, 30; and sexuality, 23, 65; subject critique, 11, 30

Isozaki, Arata, 114

I Thought I Was Seeing Convicts (*Ich glaubte Gefangene zu sehen,* Farocki), 41

Jaeger, Werner, 36

Jakobson, Roman: and aphasia, 67–68; and metaphor and metonymy, 48–50, 65–66

Jameson, Fredric, 10

Jamila, the Algerian (Chahine), 146n77

Jeanne Dielman, 23, Quai du Commerce, 1080 Bruxelles (Akerman), 11, 42–43, 59–63, 66–67, 140n65

Jetée, La (Marker), 124

Journey to the East (Le Corbusier), 96

Kames, Lord Henry Home, 149n37

Kant, Immanuel, 87

Kratylos, 131n35

Krauss, Rosalind, 7, 60, 62, 121–22, 151n67

labor, 39–69; division of, 50, 57, 66; domestic, 11, 27, 41–46, 51, 53, 61, 63, 66; feminization of, 43; immaterial, 40, 44, 135n4, 136n6; industrial, 39–42, 56, 65, 67, 135n4; and metonymy, 44–45, 48–50, 57, 59, 62, 63–69; montage and, 39–51; "of the head and the heart" (Hardt and Negri), 44; uninterrupted, 43, 72

Lacan, Jacques, 18–19, 25, 48, 50, 66; on metaphor and metonymy, 48, 50; and mirror image, 6, 15–16, 23

Lacoue-Labarthe, Philippe, 18, 35, 132n42; on rhuthmos/rhythm, 5–7, 11, 20–24, 30–32, 80–81, 91–92

Lang, Fritz. See *Metropolis*; *Odyssey*

Laplanche, Jean, 115, 145n66

Leclaire, Serge, 115

Le Corbusier. See *Journey to the East*

Lefebvre, Henri, 114
Leroi-Gourhan, André, 72
Leucippus, 20
Levine, Carole, 10
LeWitt, Sol, 20
life, 13–38; and fantasy, 6, 27, 104–5, 115; and fluidity, 13–19; forms of, 3–4, 7, 11, 32–38, 63, 116; and idiorrythmy (Barthes), 6, 27, 104; of images, 1, 4, 10–11, 27, 33, 38; "nymphal" (Agamben), 19, 33, 35; rhythm of, 19–24; virtual, 6. *See also* Barthes, Roland; being
line, 43, 116–17, 125; boundary, 1, 60, 102–4, 111; color and, 8, 12, 94–96, 145n47; in *Contempt*, 85; of flight, 47, 126. *See also* perspective
Lumière Brothers, 89. See also *Employees Leaving the Lumière Factory*
Lynch, David, 5. See also *Mulholland Drive*
Lyotard, Jean-François, 2–3, 122

Mallarmé, Stéphane, 9, 84
Man with a Movie Camera (Vertov), 11, 39–41, 57–59
Marazzi, Christian, 43–44
Margulies, Ivone, 42–43, 60, 61
Marker, Chris. See *Jetée, La*
Mayne, Judith, 140n65
Mbembe, Achille, 103
McRobie, Angela, 90
measure: "beyond," 3–4, 19, 38, 44–45, 56, 137n18; and CGS system, 26, 132n49; and domestic labor, 43–44; establishing, 17, 62, 113; *metron*, 5, 6, 22; "outside," 4–5, 44–45, 128n9, 137n18; and rhuthmos/rhythm, 4, 6, 35–36, 37, 50, 131n30; of time, 7, 37–38, 45, 76, 81–82, 122, 125, 150n42
Mecca Flats (Chicago), 102, *108*, 110–11, 117, 119
medium: digital, 2, 12, 17, 112–13; and enclosure, 99–107. *See also* cinema; photography
Meisel, Edmund, 101
memory, 71–98, 113, 120; auratic, 75–80, 82, 89, 91, 93, 98; and color, 83–88, 97; impersonal, 86, 92; involuntary, 79–80, 91; montage and, 71–76; power of, 89, 92; rhythm of, 80–83, 86; vision and, 81, 83
Merleau-Ponty, Maurice, 8, 95–96, 119. *See also* flesh
Meschonnic, Henri, 6, 7
metaphor, 8–9, 11, 95; metonymy and, 48–51, 61–62, 64–68. *See also* equivalence; hypermetaphoricity; substitution
metonymy, 11, 44, 57, 58–59, 95; beyond, 63–69; metaphor and, 48–51, 61–62, 64–68
Metropolis (Lang), 39
Metz, Christian, 49, 138nn32–33
Mezzadra, Sandro, 103
Michelson, Annette, 45
Mies van der Rohe. *See* Crown Hall, Illinois Institute of Technology
Milk (Wall), 17–18
mirror image, 6, 15–16, 23–24, 28, 130n14
modernism, 93, 109, 121–23. *See also* Crown Hall, Illinois Institute of Technology
modernity, 40, 76–77, 78

Modern Times (Chaplin), 39, 56
mode, 24, 32, 38, 75; of being, 3–4, 18–19, 24, 26–27, 35–36, 87, 102; of symbolic production, 49–50, 66, 75
modulation, 8, 35–37, 54, 95, 104, 113, 122; of the sensible, 11–12, 75, 87–88, 118–19
montage, 39–51; in Benjamin, 144n48; in Eisenstein, 68, 100–101, 106–7; in Godard, 93–94, 146n78; history of, 71–76; in *L'Atalante*, 19; in *Mulholland Drive*, 89–90, 92–93; rhythm of, 76, 78, 82, 101–2, 107, 125. *See also* editing; soft montage
movement, 42, 151n67; of bodies, 3, 35–36, 39; rhuthmos as, 131n30; rhythm as, 5–6; time subordinated to, 9, 33–34; of waves, 16–17. *See also* dance; gesture
Mowitt, John, 81–82
Mulholland Drive (Lynch), 11–12, 75, 82–83, 88–93; and aura, 89, 91–92
Mulvey, Laura, 83
Munro, Thomas, 8
Muraro, Luisa, 11, 45, 50, 68; on metaphor and metonymy, 44, 57, 65–66, 137n21
music, 3, 6–8, 31, 35–36, 81, 86, 89–90, 92, 112–14, 116, 125, 132n42. *See also* dance; sound
Muybridge, Eadweard, 34
My American Uncle (*Mon oncle d'Amérique*, Resnais), 71, 73–75, 97–98

Nancy, Jean-Luc, 97, 152n75
Negri, Antonio, 4, 44, 137n18
Neorealism, Italian, 5, 11, 41–45, 53, 58
Nielsen, Brett, 103
Nietzsche, Friedrich, 104
Number Two (*Numéro deux*, Godard), 11, 45–47, 50, 141n76, 141n81

Obsession (*Ossessione*, Visconti), 42, 51, 58
Odyssey (Lang), 85
ontology, 4, 7–9, 97; of the flesh, 2–3, 9–10, 95; modal, 11, 35
Ophuls, Max. *See Plaisir, Le*
origin, 5, 17, 31, 82, 88, 128n10
Osborne, Peter, 105, 118

Paisan (Rossellini), 96
Paracelsus, 34–35
perception, 4, 16, 36, 101; acoustic, 23, 28, 82, 92; auratic, 11–12, 75, 77–79, 87, 92, 98; cinematic, 73–79; oneiric, 58, 86–87; and time, 9, 55, 79–80, 120; visual, 16, 23, 59, 92, 101, 114, 116, 125, 139n54
perspective, 9, 107, 111, 114, 117
Philosophy in the Kitchen (Torlasco), 42
photography, 79, 130n20, 150n38, 151n67; and instantaneity, 12, 126; and rhythm, 105, 109–20; and water, 16–18, 130n18. *See also* image(s)
Piranesi, Giovanni Battista, 99–100, 147n10
Plaisir, Le (Ophuls), 98
Plato, 25, 36; and choral art, 21–22, 34, 102; and rhuthmos, 5–6, 19–24, 34–35
Plonowska Ziarek, Ewa, 10, 16, 25, 37

poetry, 5, 8, 19, 31, 80, 83–84, 110; and prosody, 6–7, 143n26
politics, 5, 77, 105, 132n42, 144n48; anti-identarian, 25–26; and biopolitics, 10, 137n18; of memory, 82–83, 102, 120
potentiality, 2, 5, 10, 97–98, 137n25; and gesture, 36–38, 54–57, 59; in *Numéro deux*, 66, 69; rhuthmos as, 54–55, 146n78; in *Umberto D.*, 62. *See also* becoming
power, 23, 44, 56, 63, 96, 100, 115–16, 129n4; of cinema, 1, 28, 83–84, 91; of interruption, 35, 36, 38; of invention, 57, 66, 67; and resistance, 60–61, 116, 129n24; rhythm's relationship to, 27, 101–2
Prairie (Burgin), 102–3, 104–5, 109–20, 126; stills from, *107, 108*
pre-Socratic philosophy, 5, 9–10, 18–19, 80. *See also* Aristotle; Plato
Proust, Marcel, 9, 84, 93
psychoanalysis, 11, 15, 23, 32, 48, 78, 102, 115; and death drive, 31–32, 62. *See also* unconscious, the

Reed, Carol. *See Third Man, The*
Reik, Theodor, 30–31, 80–81, 91–92
repetition, 2–3, 8, 37, 69, 80–81, 92, 140n65; compulsion, 25, 30–31, 32, 62, 122
representation, 16, 42, 50, 95, 97, 106, 136n9. *See also* tableau
resistance, 37, 44, 50, 110, 111, 128n24; cinematic, 14, 83, 129n4; rhuthmos as, 55–56, 116
Resnais, Alain. *See My American Uncle; Same Old Song*
rhein. *See* flowing; rhuthmos

rhuthmos, 25–26, 54, 80, 87–88; and atomism, 20; aura as, 80, 82, 87; etymology of (Benveniste), 5, 19–24, 35–36; as form of life, 11, 19, 32–33, 63; and metonymy, 68–69; notion of, 18–22, 45, 75, 103–4, 114, 115, 131n29; as resistance, 55–56, 116. *See also* configuration; flowing: "manner of"
rhythm, 5, 55, 75, 87, 90, 92; being as, 3–4, 7–9, 26; as form, 36, 122, 131n29; irregular, 11, 77, 88; of labor, 40, 43–45; and measure, 4, 6, 36–37, 50, 131n30; and memory, 80–83, 86; as method of analysis (Lefebvre), 114–15; and montage, 76, 78, 82, 101–2, 107, 125; as ontological force, 4, 8, 12, 25, 97, 146n78; as "order in movement" (Plato), 5, 21–22; percussive, 32, 78, 81–82, 90; photography as, 105, 109–20; psychoanalysis and, 18–19, 23. *See also* aura; dance; idiorrhythmy; rhuthmos
Ricci Lucchi, Angela, 146n68
Rilke, Rainer Maria, 93
Rimbaud, Arthur, 7–8, 94
Rodowick, D. N., 112, 118
Rome Open City (Rossellini), 152n82
Rossellini, Roberto, 83. *See Europe '51; Paisan; Rome Open City*

Saarinen, Eero, 110
Sakai, Naoki, 121, 152n75
Same Old Song (*On connaît la chanson*, Resnais), 74
Sauvanet, Pierre, 20, 22
Schadt, Thomas. *See Berlin: Symphony of a City*

schema, 19–21, 23, 25, 35–36, 131n30, 132n39. *See also* form
Schor, Naomi, 111, 149n37
Scott, Ridley. See *Blade Runner*
Sekula, Allan, 119
Senghor, Léopold Sédar, 7–9
sensible, the, 3–5, 9–10, 22, 24, 37, 77, 81; modulation of, 11–12, 75, 87–88, 118–19; rhuthmos as arrangement of, 25–26
Serres, Michel, 6, 129n5, 131nn29–30
Shelley, Percy, 58
Silences of the Palace, The (Tlatli), 146n77
Silverman, Kaja, 14, 17, 46–47, 63–64, 69, 129n4, 130nn19–20, 141n81
Simon, Claire. See *At All Costs*
Simondon, Gilbert, 142n12
simultaneity, 9, 12, 42, 46, 105, 106, 119–21; as difference, 12, 21, 126; and succession, 29, 48, 56, 67, 114–15, 117, 123
Sirk, Douglas. See *Written on the Wind*
Snow, Michael, 96
soft montage, 37, 59, 62, 63; in Farocki, 45–51, 47; and split-screen technique, 30, 64, 67, 69, 137n25
Solaris (Tarkovsky), 18
Sophocles, 20
sound, 13, 27, 30, 76, 82, 92, 101, 124, 133n54; and image, 31–32, 82. *See also* music
space, 25, 77, 105, 120; ordering of time and, 10, 22, 40, 63, 88–93, 103–4, 113–14, 116–17, 121–22. *See also* border
spectatorship, 3, 5, 40, 78, 84, 91, 101, 124; and consciousness, 73, 153n84; creativity of, 1–2, 97; in Godard's films, 69, 84, 86; in *Mulholland Drive*, 91–92
Spinoza, Baruch, 136n9
Steichen, Edward, 119
Stevens, Wallace, 31
Steyerl, Hito, 135n4
Stiegler, Bernard, 11, 72–75, 84, 92, 142n12, 144n48, 145n67, 153n84
subject, 10–11, 30, 33–35, 54, 84, 102, 120; formation of, 81–82, 116; intentional, 11, 60, 75, 84; and object, 8–9, 12, 14, 18–19, 60, 62, 65, 73–75, 77, 79, 82, 87. *See also* consciousness
subjectivity, 4, 11, 103, 152n74; and rhythm, 6, 75, 81, 92, 120
substitution, 2, 45, 65, 67, 82, 119, 137n21. *See also* metaphor; metonymy
succession, 102, 152n81, 153n88; simultaneity and, 29, 48, 67, 114–15, 117, 123. *See also* continuity
superimposition, 3, 19, 86, 90, 93, 109, 117, 119
synchronization, 72–73, 121
syncopation, 82, 89–90, 109. *See also* beat; cadence; dance

tableau, 105–6, 109–12. *See also* enclosure; frame
Tafuri, Manfredo, 100
Tarkovsky, Andrei. See *Solaris*
Tashlin, Frank. See *Girl Can't Help It, The*
Taubin, Amy, 93–94
temporality, 15–16, 35–36, 79, 107, 112–13, 119, 122, 147n9, 153n88; of fantasy, 115, 120, 126; of the unconscious, 19, 78. *See also* time

Third Man, The (Reed), 57
time, 10, 25, 58, 72, 77, 105, 119–20, 136n9, 153n84, 153n86; images of, 34, 42, 53, 55, 86; movement through, 33–34; photography and, 12, 18, 112, 118, 125–26, 150n38. *See also* continuity; discontinuity; duration; instantaneity; space: ordering of time and; temporality
Tlatli, Moufida. See *Silences of the Palace, The*
Torlasco, Domietta, 4, 95. See also *Philosophy in the Kitchen*
Tourneur, Jacques. See *Berlin Express*
Two or Three Things I Know about Her (Godard), 42–43, 62

Umberto D. (De Sica), 11, 42–43, 45, 51–57, 58, 60, 62; stills from, 52, 53
unconscious, the, 12, 76; and memory, 19, 31, 73–74, 119. *See also* consciousness; psychoanalysis

Valéry, Paul, 86–87
Varda, Agnes, 7
Vertigo (Hitchcock), 29–30, 96
Vertov, Dziga, 45, 47, 51, 139n54. See also *Man with a Movie Camera*
Vigo, Jean, 5. See also *Atalante, L'*; *Zero for Conduct*

Viola, Bill, 33
Virilio, Paul, 119
Virno, Paolo, 102
Visconti, Luchino. See *Earth Trembles, The*; *Obsession*
vision, 2, 14, 17–19, 81, 100, 113, 119, 121–23, 126; auratic, 78–79, 91; touch and, 95–96; as *voyance*, 8–9, 19

Wall, Jeff, 16–18, 112–13, 130n20
Warburg, Aby, 10, 34–35, 134n69
water, 35, 38, 96, 130n18; motion of, 13–19, 27; in photographic process, 112–13, 130n18. *See also* flowing
Water and Dreams (Bachelard), 18
Winnicott, D. W., 113
Wiskus, Jessica, 7, 8, 9–10
Woolf, Virginia, 28, 66
Workers Leaving the Factory (*Arbeiter verlassen die Fabrik*, Farocki), 39–40, 42
Written on the Wind (Sirk), 1–2

Zavattini, Cesare, 53, 55
Zero for Conduct (*Zéro de conduite*, Vigo), 26–27

DOMIETTA TORLASCO is a critical theorist, filmmaker, and associate professor in the Department of French and Italian and the Comparative Literary Studies Program at Northwestern University. She is author of *The Heretical Archive: Digital Memory at the End of Film* (Minnesota, 2013) and *The Time of the Crime: Phenomenology, Psychoanalysis, Italian Film.* Her recent video essays screened at the Walker Art Center in Minneapolis and the Museum of Contemporary Art in Los Angeles.